THE
"UNHEALED"
BELIEVER

THE
"UNHEALED"
BELIEVER

What to Do When You've Done It All

REDEMPTION PRESS

TERESA HOUGHTELING

Published by Redemption Press, PO Box 427, Enumclaw, WA 98022.

Toll-Free (844) 2REDEEM (273-3336)

Redemption Press is honored to present this title in partnership with the author. The views expressed or implied in this work are those of the author. Redemption Press provides our imprint seal representing design excellence, creative content, and high-quality production.

Unless otherwise indicated, all Scripture quotations are taken from the New King James Version (NKJV). Copyright © 1982 by Thomas Nelson, Inc. Used by permission. All rights reserved.

Scripture quotations marked KJV are taken from the Holy Bible, King James Version, © 1979, 1980, 1982 by Thomas Nelson, Inc., Publishers. Used by permission.

Scripture quotations marked NLT are from taken the Holy Bible, New Living Translation, copyright © 1996, 2004, 2015 by Tyndale House Foundation. Used by permission of Tyndale House Publishers Inc., Carol Stream, Illinois 60188. All rights reserved.

Scripture quotations marked MSG are taken from The Message, copyright © 1993, 2002, 2018 by Eugene H. Peterson. Used by permission of NavPress. All rights reserved. Represented by Tyndale House Publishers, Inc.

Scripture quotations marked AMP are taken from the Amplified Bible. Copyright © 1954, 1958, 1962, 1964, 1965, 1987 by The Lockman Foundation. Used by permission.

Scripture quotations marked NABRE are taken from the New American Bible, revised edition © 2010, 1991, 1986, 1970 Confraternity of Christian Doctrine, Inc., Washington, DC All Rights Reserved. No part of this work may be reproduced or transmitted in any form or by any means, electronic or mechanical, including photocopying, recording, or by any information storage and retrieval system, without permission in writing from the copyright owner.

Scripture quotations marked NIV are taken from the Holy Bible, New International Version®, NIV® Copyright ©1973, 1978, 1984, 2011 by Biblica, Inc.® Used by permission. All rights reserved worldwide.

ISBN: 978-1-64645-203-3 (Paperback)
978-1-64645-204-0 (ePub)
978-1-64645-205-7 (Mobi)

Library of Congress Catalog Card Number: 2020913105

To Patrick, my love.
From all the places we've been,
to all the places we've yet to go,
one thing remains unchanged … I love you.

CONTENTS

FOREWORD

I love Teresa's healing testimony. She chose the best way to receive a healing from the Lord. It's not the only way, but it's the best way.

Many people believe God can heal, and some will even go as far as to believe that it's God's will to heal, but few know how to receive that healing on their own. They have to have someone else join their faith with them or they totally rely on the supernatural gifts of healings or miracles. There is no bad way to get healed, but there is a way which is better than others.

Jesus has already provided all the healing we will ever need. By His stripes we were healed (1 Peter 2:24). It's a done deal that is available to anyone for the taking. But most people see healing as something that is yet to be done. They pray and then passively wait on the Lord to accomplish it. They will say they are waiting on God to heal them, but in truth, God is waiting on them to receive what He has already provided.

Teresa got this truth. She quit begging for healing and started taking her authority as a believer and commanding what Jesus had already provided to come to pass. It was a process and took some time. But because she received by her faith, her healing is secure. She doesn't have to wait until the next anointed man or woman of God comes to town to get what she needs. She's already got it.

The same truths that set Teresa free from years of chronic pain and suffering will work for you. Teresa shares step by step how the Lord brought her to this freedom, and God is no respecter of persons. What He has done for Teresa He has already done for you. You just need to learn how to receive. That's what this book is all about.

~Andrew Wommack

A SPECIAL NOTE

From Daniel Amstutz

In the book *The "Unhealed" Believer*, Teresa Houghteling passionately shares her healing journey with the hope that you will learn from her story and rise up and take what is rightfully yours as a believer in Jesus Christ! She invites you into her experience to let you know that healing has already been provided, just like forgiveness has, and how you can have the knowledge of God's Word revealed to you personally, by the Holy Spirit, and have your own revelation (revealed knowledge) of healing to help you take hold of what has already been done for you in Christ. Teresa says, "Once you take hold of your healing, nothing can ever take that away from you," and I agree!

As an instructor at Charis Bible College and Director of The Healing School and Charis Worship Arts, I met Teresa as a student in 2013 and watched her take hold of the Word of God in her life and walk through much of the process that she shares in this powerful but easy to read book. I will never forget the day that she told me she had received her healing! It was a day of much rejoicing, and that rejoicing has never stopped! Her testimony is encouraging, practical, and powerful!

Teresa is transparent in sharing her story and because of it, she presents a "you can do this" attitude no matter what you've gone through! Through pain, betrayal, shame, and unforgiveness, not realizing she was living with a stolen identity, she had opened some doors to sickness and disease that she thought she would have to manage for the rest of her life.

Teresa shares how Jesus didn't tell us He came to manage our sickness, but rather how He came to take sickness away! He carried it so we wouldn't have to carry it in us!

Once Teresa discovered how much her heavenly Father loved her personally and unconditionally, she started to receive what God had already provided through Christ. Teresa shares how finally knowing she was unconditionally loved by God Himself caused the faith she already had to come alive in her, becoming effective in her and through her like she had never known. The truth she learned set her free! She discovered that faith doesn't move God; faith responds to what the grace of God has already provided.

Jesus didn't say on the cross, it was **almost** finished. He said, "It is finished!" What amazing love.

Enjoy this powerful journey from sickness and disease to healing and wellness as Teresa shares powerful truths about how you can receive your healing and help others receive theirs as well. Receive what is already yours.

Teresa says, "I know who I am, I know what I have, and I know how I got it." I love that!

~Daniel Amstutz
Director of Charis Worship Arts and The Healing School

ACKNOWLEDGMENTS

One of the blessings of writing this book has been to know Dee Worley. As my editor, I am forever grateful for her talent, wisdom, and experience as she has walked me through the writing and publishing process. She selflessly donated her time to make this book what it is today.

Dee, you are not just my editor, but you are my friend. I couldn't have accomplished this without you. You are deeply appreciated and loved.

To my best friend, Sandy Fifer. There are no words to express how much your friendship means to me. No matter where we go, or the physical distance between us, my heart is always with you.

And to the King of kings and Lord of lords, You have been faithful … and You have done it.

INTRODUCTION

As a believer, there are few things less frustrating than knowing God can heal, knowing He is willing to heal, knowing He has *already* healed through the finished work of the cross, knowing the Scriptures to back it up, but still not seeing that healing in your body. For many years, I *tried* to get healed. I *willed* myself to be healed, and it just didn't work. In all honesty, I finally got tired of the disappointment that came with believing, so I gave in to pain and disease. I accepted that it was just something I had to live with for the rest of my life, and I learned how to cope with the symptoms.

For thirteen years, I lived with the diseases that were slowly killing me, not knowing what else I could do. I had done everything I knew to do. That is the position I walked in for the majority of my Christian life until something changed—in me—October 2013.

During a bout with the worst respiratory sickness I had ever faced, a targeted anger and determination rose within me. I was righteously angry (indignant, actually) that I wasn't walking in health as God's Word said I should be, and I was determined to take hold of all of the benefits He said I should have, including walking in the healing He provided for everyone.

Six months later, on March 13, 2014, I received my complete healing.

Don't worry. That's not a spoiler alert. There's a lot of backstory in that sentence. The backstory's got the gold.

The bigger point is that even though I knew the Word said I was healed from the very day I put my trust in Jesus and accepted Him as my Lord and Savior (which was before I got sick), I didn't know how to get what I knew in my head to become alive and activated in my body. I knew the Word, but I didn't know how to receive what He had promised.

This book outlines the process I went through and the revelation I received during the six months that ultimately led to my healing.

It's important for you to understand that there is no formula for receiving the healing that was fully bought and paid for you to receive. And yes, I intentionally phrased that sentence exactly that way. Healing is not to be dispensed from God to you. It has already been dispensed. Healing is for you to receive. That's an important distinction that keeps many frustrated believers locked out of the life they want to be living.

So, while I stand by my claim that there's no formula, I believe there are some basic principles that, if applied consistently, will always result in every believer receiving their blood-bought healing—every time.

Yep. I said it. I know it's a definitive statement. I'm not taking it back.

How do I know that, and how can I so confidently say it?

Because everything I did to receive my healing came straight from the Word of God. There was nothing fancy, nothing mystical. I simply did what Father (that's how I regularly refer to Him) told me to do. I did it with all of my heart. And, with a little perseverance, the healing I already had manifested physically in my body.

After all the years of strain, struggle, trying, and forcing, it really did end up being just that simple. My receiving healing was not just for me; it was for me to share with you so you can also be free from what binds you. Matthew 10:27 says, "Whatever I tell you in the dark, speak in the light; and what you hear in the ear, preach on the housetops" (NKJV).

I pray these words, shouted out from deep within me, will inspire you to achieve your own victory. As you read these pages, I pray that a renewed enthusiasm awakens in you. I hope that enthusiasm pushes you to have a relentless attitude of expectant victory over whatever sickness or disease you're struggling with, that a passion would stir up in you to take hold of God's best for you, and that you would rise up and claim what is rightfully yours as a believer in Jesus Christ.

What's rightfully yours is divine healing.

I invite you to learn from my journey. It is a journey that begins with an unhealed believer (there really is no such thing as an unhealed believer, but that's what I thought I was) and concludes in total, complete, permanent healing.

I am sharing *how* I received the revelation of healing so you can get your own revelation: the revelation *you* need. It is my heart's desire that, as you read the following pages, strongholds will be broken, incorrect thinking will be exposed, your heart will be changed, and you will be healed.

If you just read what is written, don't apply it to your life and make it your own, these words will only serve as regurgitated revelation, and nothing will change for you. *The key to receiving is to take it and let Father make it yours.* I believe His favorite way for His children to receive healing is through His Word, because once you get a revelation of His Word and take hold of your healing, nothing can ever take that away from you.

I'm going to show you how to do it.

"Darkness cannot drive out darkness:
only light can do that."
Martin Luther King Jr.

CHAPTER ONE

Darkness Ruled

'm just like you. I'm not a spiritual "super-duper." I have lived far from a pure, holy, God-focused existence for the majority of my life. In fact, for a long time—before I finally admitted that I was making a mess of things by trying to be and do it all on my own—my life was quite the disaster. By not surrendering my life to God, I was trapping myself in a vicious cycle that had made me numb to the effects sin and rebellion were having on me (and others connected to me).

My goal with this book is to be completely transparent. I'm sharing the good, the bad, and the unmentionable. I believe there's freedom in confession, and James 5:16 confirms this belief: "Confess your trespasses to one another, and pray for one another, that you may be healed. The effective, fervent prayer of a righteous man avails much" (NKJV). To that end, I am humbly admitting my faults, so you know exactly where I came from, and what I had to get through to enjoy the benefits of where I am today. By the end of this leg of the journey, I want you to be able to say, "If she can get it, I can get it!"

Again, there is nothing special about me. I simply took God's Word at face value, believed every word of it, and did what it said to do. That was—and is—my "formula." This is how I win in life.

Ready to win?

My journey to living in healing and wholeness began when I was a child. (Don't be discouraged—your journey doesn't have to take as long as mine did!) I was saved at a very young age thanks to a dedicated neighbor who picked my three siblings and me up on Sundays for church. I was so young, in fact, that I hardly remember a Sunday school teacher leading me in a prayer to accept Jesus into my heart. The memory is fuzzy, but it happened.

Shortly after that, the lives of my family members were forever changed when my oldest sibling, Jeff, died in a car accident. I was five years old, and too young to really understand what had happened to my big brother, but I sure did feel the void of his absence.

Jeff's death was the catalyst that changed my dad from a hard-working farmer to a dedicated man of God. Through his mourning, his heart was transformed and he was called into full-time ministry. He uprooted and moved us from a working farm in a tiny town in Iowa to the big city (it was to us, anyway) of Broken Arrow, Oklahoma, where he attended Rhema Bible Training College. The trajectory of our lives was radically rerouted by that decision. We went from being "holiday heathens" (you should laugh at that) to never-miss-a-Sunday church folk. Our lives became all about God and what we could do for Him (the operative word here is *for*). During dad's two years of study there, we attended (then Pastor) Bob Yandian's church, Grace (now pastored by his son Rob), and I was baptized in the Spirit with the evidence of speaking in tongues. (There are two books I would highly recommend if you are unsure about this "speaking in tongues" thing or if you are struggling with receiving your own prayer language. They are *Why Tongues* by Kenneth E. Hagin[1] and *The New You & The Holy Spirit* by Andrew Wommack.[2] Both books plainly spell out why this is such an important gift—for *every* believer—from the Holy Spirit, and will lead you in receiving it.)

I remember the Sunday School teacher leading us in a prayer as I stood in front of her with a bunch of other kids. I was around seven years old at the time, and I had my eyes shut as tight as I could because I didn't know what was going on, or what was going to happen. But what I *did* know was that if the Bible said I should speak in tongues—which it does in many places including Acts 2:4, 10:44–46, and 19:6—then I should speak in tongues. After all, I heard my dad doing it all the time, and he always seemed to be in a better mood afterward. So it couldn't be all that bad, could it? Little did I know, that gift, the gift of the Holy Spirit, would be a vital part of not only my life, but a vital part in my healing journey.

After dad's graduation from Rhema Bible Training College, we moved back to Iowa, and I began my life as a "PK": a preacher's kid. Growing up with that label was not easy. There was a lot of pressure from adults to be good, and a lot of pressure from kids to be bad. If I didn't go along with the kids, I was labeled "Miss Goody-Two-Shoes." If I did go along with them, I was confronted with the disapproval of the adults.

I felt like I was constantly in a no-win situation. I was expected to go to church every Sunday, even if I was sick. In those instances, my mom would say, "Oh, you're throwing up? Take a shower, get dressed, and you'll feel better. It's almost time for church." I had to dress a certain way. "That skirt is way too short! No jeans on Sunday!" I couldn't listen to the music my friends enjoyed. Do this. Don't do that. As a teenager, I felt like the Word had created a prison for me to live in, and if I attempted to step outside the walls of the prison, I would be punished and promptly returned to the cell. (That's what is commonly called "being grounded" for those of you who have forgotten.)

I couldn't have defined it then, but those rules that were meant for my good and to protect me had turned into legalism in my mind. Someone once defined legalism like this: "Rules without relationship leads to rebellion." As soon as I left home for college, I would prove his statement to be right. I had tons of rules about living holy and absolutely no relationship with Jesus. That could only lead to one thing: rebellion. It was inevitable.

That rules-without-relationship dynamic was evident when I was sixteen and had gotten in a bad car accident. I was alone in the car when it happened, and the first thing I did after the accident was turn the radio station because I was listening to secular music. I had just crashed into the back end of a stopped truck (with my parents' brand new Caprice Classic and on the first night they let me drive alone after getting my license) at about fifty miles an hour, and the first thing that occurred to me was I was doing something I shouldn't have been doing: I was listening to secular music. So, rather than being concerned about the car accident that had just happened (or if I was completely intact, or whether or not the car was going to explode), my first reaction was to turn the station because I didn't want my dad to know I was listening to something other than Christian music.

Rules without relationship leads to rebellion.

I felt such intense pressure to be perfect, most of which was self-imposed, and being a Christian became a performance.

That was how it felt.

A curtain went up and I was standing alone in the middle of a large stage with a spotlight shining brightly on me. There was nowhere to hide. No matter where I turned or what I did, that spotlight followed me. Every flaw was out there for the world to see, and the world was full of harsh critics. I felt as if I was perpetually on that stage, naked and with every imperfection and shortcoming exposed. I could not live up to the standards of either the audience or myself.

Looking back on that time in my life, I know my parents were just trying to raise me right by teaching me solid biblical ethics and morals. As many young people do, I interpreted their well-meaning instruction as rules and regulations, all of which subjected me to punishment if broken. Far worse than any physical punishment they could have given me was my knowing I had disappointed them. I hated their rules, but I still wanted them to be proud of me. Knowing I had hurt them or that I had failed was harsher punishment than anything else I could have imagined. They didn't need to punish me. I punished myself. I thought I needed to be perfect to make them happy. I saw this same pattern repeat itself for many years in my relationship with my heavenly Father: try hard to please Him; punish myself when I fail.

That misinterpretation caused me to run from Christianity as soon as I had the chance. However, as a proverbial self-proclaimed prodigal child who found my way back home, I am thankful that my parents exposed me to the truth of God's Word and took the time to instill those ethics and morals in me. I know it was the seeds they planted during those early years, as well as their prayers of intercession as I journeyed out on my own, that brought me back from a very dangerous place later in life.

In case you missed it, that was for anyone with their own prodigal child: keep praying and keep sowing those godly seeds. They may be able to run from you. They may be able to run from their upbringing. They may be able to run from the church. But they cannot outrun your prayers. God's Word will accomplish what it was set out to do. Your prayers are invaluable to your child whether they know it or not. Don't give up on them. I'm living proof—prayer works. Thanks, Mom and Dad.

When I graduated high school and left for college in 1992, I was like many people out there after years of living with a performance mentality: I was tired of trying to be "a good Christian." I was tired of going to church and putting on a smile I didn't feel, being the perfect "PK" and trying to please God. I was tired of reading a Bible I didn't understand. I was tired of being nice to people at church that I didn't like, when in reality, I felt like slapping them.

I was tired of trying to be who I thought I was supposed to be, and I was even more tired of trying to be what I thought others thought I should be. Every girl "PK" at some point believes she is supposed to become a pastor's wife and play the piano during praise and worship.

No way. Fat chance. Wasn't happening.

I was burned out.

You might wonder how that could happen to someone who grew up under the truth of the Word. My answer is simple: I never made the Word my own.

Rules without relationship leads to rebellion.

The Bible was just words on a page to me. Nothing more. I was saved and filled with the Spirit, but those purported life-altering decisions I'd made didn't mean anything to me.

I was saved and stuck.

So I quit. I quit going to church. I quit praying, even the little bit that I had been (which was usually only in a crisis and when I needed something from God ASAP). I quit reading my Bible. I quit being nice to people. I dove head-first into the world (which is the opposite of the way, the truth, and the light), and I attempted to do life on its terms.

Here's the rub: At first, life was much easier for me. I seemed happier. I felt free. I was doing what I wanted to do and what I thought was best for my future. I thought I'd finally gotten control of my own life and there was nobody there to tell me what to do, how to act, or who to be. I threw off my identity as a Christian and began trying desperately to fit in with "normal people."

In college I met new people and got into the party

scene. This was quite the opposite of middle school and high school where I was picked on mercilessly because of the three strikes I had against me:

1. I was a "PK."
2. We moved every couple of years to start a new church, so I never really made friends.
3. I had terrible cystic acne from a very young age.

Those three things, coupled with the cruelty of kids, contributed to my being an introvert—until I got to college. In college, people invited me to parties (a totally foreign experience for me, by the way). I jumped right in. That reckless abandon led to much heartbreak as I was used and then discarded by many "friends." The pattern was: I would meet a new friend. We would party together. She would meet a boy. I never saw her again. Repeat. I was invited to the party so she wouldn't have to go alone, but I was expendable. In the beginning, I really didn't care. I was just happy to be invited. After a while, it hurt. Boys would show interest, but as soon as I put the brakes on, they wanted nothing to do with me. More hurt. Would I *ever* be good enough for *anybody*?

College is also where I met my first husband. (Yes, I said my first.) He wasn't like the other boys whose intent was to use me and throw me away. He truly loved me for who I was on the inside. He could see past my acne. We had a very brief courtship and married quickly. He made me feel accepted and loved, and I thought those were the sole requirements for a marriage to work. He joined the

Navy shortly after we got married, and so began long periods of our being apart.

By the third year of that marriage, I was extremely lonely and had an affair with a man while my then-husband was on a long deployment. When he returned home, I told him of the affair and asked for a divorce. He wanted to reconcile, but I told myself I didn't love him anymore, that I never really loved him, and I pushed for the divorce. My parents came to visit to try and talk some sense into me, but my mind was made up. I think deep down I wanted to save the marriage, but every time I looked at him I couldn't get past the overwhelming guilt and shame I felt for betraying him. After the divorce, my eyes were eventually opened to what a truly good man he was, and the way I treated him weighed on me heavily for many years.

How could I ever forgive myself?

The reality is, I didn't forgive myself. Not then, anyway. Instead, I rationalized my choices, buried those feelings, and moved on (or so I told myself).

Before the divorce was finalized, I met my second husband. (Yes, I said my second husband.) We dated for three years before we married, and by the world's standards we were living The American Dream. We were both making good money. We drove nice cars, had built our first home, and threw great parties. I was even training for a marathon. Everything was great until one morning in 2001.

Psalm 40:2–5 (NLT)

"He lifted me out of the pit of despair,
out of the mud and the mire.
He set my feet on solid ground
and steadied me as I walked along.
He has given me a new song to sing,
a hymn of praise to our God.
Many will see what he has done and be
amazed.
They will put their trust in the LORD.
Oh, the joys of those who trust the LORD,
who have no confidence in the proud
or in those who worship idols.
O LORD my God, you have performed many
wonders for us.
Your plans for us are too numerous to list.
You have no equal.
If I tried to recite all your wonderful deeds,
I would never come to the end of them."

CHAPTER TWO

Light Overcomes Darkness

I woke up and couldn't get out of bed. The girl who had just run thirteen miles the week before couldn't muster up enough energy to get out of bed.

The fatigue was severe. It was as if I weighed three thousand pounds. Over the next several days, I noticed that my hair was beginning to fall out in large chunks. Severe muscle cramps at night jolted me out of my sleep. Brain fog escalated to the point that I was running through red lights. Thinking of words and forming proper sentences were difficult. I'd forget conversations I'd had just moments after having them, which created a lot of tension between my husband and me. I can't tell you how many times I heard, "But we just talked about that!" I was a nurse at the time, and I couldn't remember medication dosages I had known how to calculate like the back of my hand. Considering that I was working in the pediatric emergency room, being able to draw up medications quickly could literally be a matter of life and death.

Something was wrong.

Blood work revealed that my thyroid gland had completely shut down. The doctors said there was no cure for my condition. They prescribed medication—which, of course, required lifelong usage—that would replace the vital hormones my body was no longer producing.

That seemed an easy-enough fix, so I spent the next two years getting the thyroid medication regulated and getting used to taking my pill every day. Every now and then I would forget to take it, and within a day or two the symptoms would return with a vengeance. There was no mistaking when I hadn't taken it. I could not function normally without it.

Physically, I seemed to be doing pretty well until I started experiencing sharp pain in my right shoulder. I hadn't fallen or lifted anything heavy, and there was no explanation for the pain. Along with that pain came a rash that surfaced every time my skin was exposed to the sun, as well as my frequent catching of colds and viruses from my little patients in the emergency room.

I went back to the doctor, and they performed more blood work. These results uncovered the reason for the pain and rash symptoms, as well as the underlying reason why my thyroid gland had stopped working. It was because of an autoimmune disease called Sjögren's syndrome. My immune system was confused, and couldn't differentiate between what was good and what was bad, so its response was to destroy everything: bad and good. This meant my body was attacking its own cells and organs. It was literally killing me from the inside out. The disease initially attacks the moisture-producing glands of the body, which causes severe dry eyes and mouth.

It had progressed far beyond that in me.

Doctors said any one of my vital organs could be its

next target since it had already taken out my thyroid gland. They concluded that I'd just have to "wait and see" what it attacked next.

Wait and see?

Those three little words triggered a fear in me that haunted me for years as I vigilantly checked my organs' functions every six months. According to this prognosis, I would have to "wait and see" for the rest of my life as Sjögren's syndrome was incurable. Incurable. That is what they told me, and that is what I accepted.

They told me I needed to transfer out of the emergency room—the job I loved—because my immune system couldn't handle the constant barrage of bacteria and viruses from my patients. I transferred to the Neonatal Intensive Care Unit, the most sterile environment I could find, and began thinking about a new career. If I couldn't be in the Peds ER, then I didn't want to be a nurse any longer. The Sjögren's was running my life. I was not.

They gave me medication to regulate the joint pain, but they could do nothing to stop the disease's progression—and neither could I. I was flooded with intense fear having the knowledge that there was a self-destruct sequence that had been activated in my body, but unlike in the movies, I had no secret code word to say or big red button to press to stop it.

Not only was my physical health declining, but by December of 2007 my emotional health was hitting a wall as well. We had moved to another state for my then-husband's good job, and I hated everything about the relocation: my new job, my house, the roads, the traffic, even the grocery stores. I found myself drinking a lot of wine just to get through each day. My then-husband, who usually wanted to do everything with me, had become distant, and he was frequently gone for work.

Or so I thought.

Six months after we had moved, I was up early one morning and saw his cell phone lying on the kitchen counter. I had never searched his phone before, but I felt a strong urge to look at it. He was asleep upstairs after getting in very late, so I pulled up his photos.

What I saw broke me.

There were pictures of him living a completely separate life from the one he had been living with me. I saw him with friends I didn't know in places I had never been. One person was common in nearly all of the pictures. *It couldn't be*, I thought to myself.

That day, I learned my husband was cheating on me, and that one of the reasons he had moved us to this foreign place I'd hated was to be closer to the other person in his nefarious relationship.

But that wasn't the worst of it.

Not only was he cheating on me, but the person he was cheating with was a man. Initially, the shock of the news created a tsunami wave of emotions: rage, contempt, embarrassment, shame, and even fear. I was unimaginably blindsided by it and, quite literally, I thought my life as I knew it was a fraudulent lie. My entire world had, in an instant, completely fallen apart. I felt as if I were being slowly devoured—one bite at a time—by a ravenous force of evil with an insatiable appetite for everything I had ever believed in and trusted.

I was a shell of a person.

Then I began to blame myself. *Maybe I deserve it. After all, you reap what you sow, right?* The devil was trying to use the Word of God I knew against me. I had cheated on my first husband, so it seemed reasonably likely that I was reaping, hundredfold, what I had sown. My femininity, womanhood, and identity were under attack, and a bottomless black hole sat heavily where my heart had been.

How did I get so far down this road?

In my mind, I had no vision, no purpose, and, from all existing evidence, no reason to live. I had spent the whole of my adult life looking for happiness, and I had failed at every attempt. I'd had fleeting experiences of happiness, but they were always followed by extended periods of longing, dissatisfaction, and despair. I knew there had to be more in this life for me. I had wandered yet another lap around the proverbial mountain and was right back where I'd started: behind square one.

Is this all there is? Is this the destiny of my life? How do I go on from here?

Little did I know that what I had been searching for all along was actually a Who—not a what—and He'd been watching and waiting for me to return to Him . . . with open arms. He had been protecting me without my even realizing it, and He had been longing to comfort me when I'd failed. I discovered Scripture later that He was actually counting each of my tears as they fell. Watching, waiting, and catching my tears.

I didn't know that was happening. I didn't know what I didn't know.

What I'd believed was freedom—which in reality was

me living life for myself on my own terms—was actually bondage. I was a slave to disease, alcohol, and depression.

But, on one cold winter night in December 2007 (a few days after finding out about my then-husband's secret), I was sitting in the middle of my bed, sobbing in the dark. In a moment of complete hopelessness, I remember talking to my mom on the phone and telling her, "I feel so empty inside." The darkness in and around me was tangible. I could feel it suffocating me, crushing me. I felt it invading every cell of my body. I was in a pit I believed was too deep to get out of.

But that would all radically change in the blink of an eye.

At the point when despair had almost overtaken me, I heard a still, small voice inside me clearly say, "I have never left you, even though you have run from Me." When I heard my Father's voice—the voice I had tuned out, stopped hearing, and refused for years—the floodgates opened and I wept. His voice was gentle and loving. I had stopped listening, but He had never stopped speaking, reaching out, and urging me back to Him. Despite what I'd thought or felt, He had me and I had Him. I realized that whether or not that relationship was my experience was totally up to me. He hadn't gone anywhere; I had.

Psalm 119:130 says, "The entrance of Your words gives light." When I heard His voice, light immediately began to overcome the darkness in my life. The weight of the darkness began to lighten, and a hope stirred within me that I hadn't dared even dream of just moments before. It was right then that I knew I had a choice to make. I could continue to travel down the wide, dark path I was on alone, or I could repent and walk the narrow path with Him. I couldn't refuse this God Who was offering me the unconditional love I'd been searching for all along. I surrendered myself to His love for me and felt His arms wrap around me. Even after all I had done, He still wanted me. I repented as the darkness fled, and I dedicated myself wholly to Him. Out of my brokenness and sin, I was, finally, all-in and all His.

Romans 2:4 (AMP)

"Are you [actually] unaware or ignorant [of the fact] that God's kindness leads you to repentance [that is, to change your inner self, your old way of thinking—seek His purpose for your life]?"

CHAPTER THREE

The Overwhelming Goodness of God

God's love poured out on me in the midst of my mess made me realize there was nothing I could do to ever lose it; it was unconditional. I was free to live in His love and in His presence. My grand performances to earn His love and acceptance were actually a bitter taste in His mouth. My works were meaningless. More importantly, my mistakes had no effect on His love for me. What He wanted was my heart, my life, my commitment, and my love.

I no longer had a desire to earn—or run from—His love. He had freely, unconditionally, and with no-strings-attached given it to me. I had been so caught up in what I thought I *should* be doing, that I had missed the whole point: relationship. A real, personal, face-to-face relationship. Even now as I sit and write, when I close my eyes I can see Him holding my face in His hands, so close that I can feel His breath. Eyes locked with mine. Relationship. I had finally gotten it: He loves me. No matter what.

An understanding of Father's unconditional love for me was critical to my being able to receive from Him.

That was a major point so, in case you ran over it, I'm repeating it: *An understanding of Father's unconditional love for me was critical to my being able to receive from Him.*

I believe many people have a hard time grasping God's love for them because religion—and the world's corruption—have tainted His image to one that doesn't at all represent Him.

A word on religion.

When I say religion, I mean it as a system of rules and traditions of men that, according to Mark 7:13, "make the Word of God of no effect." Religion teaches that works are necessary in order to please God. It says that if you don't do A, B, and C, you are not worthy to receive anything from Him. In the Word, this is referred to as Old Testament law. The Israelites had 613 rules of the law (yep, way more than ten commandments) they had to keep to be in right-standing with God. That was a burden no one could bear, which was exactly the *point* of the law. He gave us the law to show us we needed a savior, that we would never be able to do it on our own.

Jesus, our Savior, was the *fulfillment* of that law. By living a sinless life (a perfect sacrifice) and dying on the cross, He fulfilled every aspect of those 613 rules (yep, including the big ten). Because of that sacrifice, we are no longer under the curse of the law, and we have entered into the new covenant of grace. We are in right-standing with God because of Jesus, not because of anything we did or can do. By requiring works to please God (which erroneously puts us back under the law), religion is saying that what Jesus did on the cross was not enough to pay the price for us. This, in turn, makes the Word of God of no effect. Think about how adding an alkaline substance to an acid will neutralize its effects. On their own, each substance is powerful, yet when they are brought together, the power of both is counteracted. In the same way, adding works to the cross diminishes its power and effect in your life.

Religion has, unfortunately, taught far too many people in the body of Christ that God's love is conditional on, among other things, their ability to earn it. Religion encourages believers to run on a mind-numbing hamster wheel of impossible-to-keep rules, not relationship. After what can seem like a lifetime of working, trying, performing, and striving to earn God's approval—and perpetually falling well short—this exercise in futility inevitably results in the frustrated question, "*What's the point?*"

The world is just as guilty of misrepresenting God as is religion. When I say *the world*, I'm referring to conventional, widely accepted, humanly conceived logic and reason. According to conventional worldview, God is relative, people must rely on themselves to create their own destiny, and truth is whatever seems (or, even worse, feels) right and fits in with a person's thinking. The world says there are no absolutes, and God's Word is just a book that can't be trusted as a reliable resource for practical life in modern society.

Based on my firsthand experience with both rejecting and accepting God's Word as the infallible truth, I confidently and definitively declare the systems of the world and religion are rooted in deception.

The acceptance of this deception causes a separation from the living God Who loves you unconditionally and sent His one-and-only Son to suffer and die to be in relationship with you.

systems of the World + religion are rooted in Deception

Back to love. Not all love is the same.

Human love, which includes a multitude of fragile strings attached, can never be compared to God's love. His love never fails. It's immeasurable and guaranteed. God loves you and longs to be a part of your life. Like any good, loving father, He wants you to live in His blessings. All the time. Every day. Without exception.

If you have children, consider how you would enhance their lives if your resources were unlimited. Ponder the truth that nothing they could ever do or say would change your love for them. We, as humans, have what we believe is unlimited love for our earthly children, but that measure of love is not even a scintilla of the boundless love our Father in heaven has for us.

Several years after my encounter with Father in 2007, I shared that pivotal moment in my life with a friend, and an even deeper understanding of Father's love and goodness manifested in me. I'd thought I understood His love completely, but I was learning that revelation comes in layers. I was learning that my revelation was only limited by the degree of my pursuit of God's truths. The more I pursued God's truths, the more revelation I received.

At lunch one day, I was telling my friend about reaching the end of myself and the choice I'd made to return to Him. My friend simply said, "His goodness brought you back." Pause—with the fork halfway to my mouth. It was like she had slapped me in the face. I had heard that Scripture before (Romans 2:4), but I'd never grasped its full meaning until that very moment. I was fully persuaded that what she'd said was the truth.

I thought about everything I had done to spite Him, and it hurt my heart to realize how I'd rejected His love for so many years. Nevertheless, I reveled in the truth that no matter what I had done, it hadn't changed His love for me. God was saying to me, as He said to Israel in Jeremiah 31:3, "I have loved you, Teresa, with an everlasting love. With unfailing love I have drawn you to Myself." He loved me. Period. He is, in a word, good.

Now Romans 2:4 (NLT) is abundantly clear to me. "Don't you see how wonderfully kind, tolerant, and patient God is with you? Does this mean nothing to you? Can't you see that his kindness is intended to turn you from your sin?"

What made this Scripture clear to me, though, was my experiencing it. I *know* this Scripture firsthand, so that confirms it as the absolute truth. Only His goodness could have drawn me back to Him and out of that pit. I had lived it, and now it was alive in me. It was God telling me I couldn't out-sin His love for me, that there was nowhere I could run that He wouldn't be waiting for me when I finally turned back. He never gave up on me. Because of His faithfulness, because of Who He is, I will go where He wants me to go, say what He wants me to say, and do what He wants me to do. It's amazing the courage and confidence you receive when you know He loves you and will never leave you.

His love and His goodness have changed me. When I look back now on that lost woman, I don't recognize her. Love has changed my countenance. It has changed how I look at myself, both inside and out. It has changed how I look at others, and it has enabled me to forgive them because of how He has forgiven me. Most importantly, His love and goodness have empowered my faith in Him because they have changed how I perceive Him as my Father. He is not sitting up in heaven keeping track of all I do wrong and looking for opportunities to punish me as I go along. He is not responsible for all the bad things that have happened in my life. He is, by nature, loving, kind, full of mercy, and has nothing but the best already planned out for me. No matter how terrible my behavior was in the past, I know without a doubt that He is not holding a single thing against me.

And He's not holding a single thing against you either. His love outweighs the sum of everything negative in your life.

Let the gravity of that statement soak in before you read on.

Psalm 56:8 (NLT)

"You keep track of all my sorrows.
You have collected all my tears in your bottle.
You have recorded each one in your book."

CHAPTER FOUR

Let It Go

After that life-altering encounter in 2007, I diligently sought Father the best I knew how at the time. I went to church every time it was open. I joined a women's Bible study and went to every event that came to town. I didn't do it to impress Him or gain His approval, but in an effort to learn more about this God Who loved me unconditionally. While I prayed daily, my intimate relationship with Him flourished. Hearing His voice was a regular occurrence again. Talking to Him throughout the whole day helped me understand that He wanted to be involved in helping me make even the most seemingly insignificant decisions. I rediscovered my prayer language and began to value it for what it was: my direct line of communication with Father (1 Corinthians 14:2 KJV). He became my life source.

There was a lot of junk in my heart and mind that needed to be exposed and eliminated. God showed me how the life experiences of being bullied, having a performance mentality, and adultery had shaped how I perceived myself and others. The fear of rejection was palpable, so I turned inward, isolating myself to protect my fragile heart and mind. The faulty belief that I would never be good enough (internally or externally) for anyone to love me again created an emotional prison, and freedom would only come by being secure in my relationship with Him. If I was secure in Him, then I could be secure in any relationship that would come after that, so I opened myself up completely to Father to help me deal with all of my junk: self-loathing, personal identity issues, fear, anger, rejection, pain, and bitterness.

What I didn't expect was the root cause of all those negative emotions. God showed me I had an unforgiving spirit. (Not spirit as in demon, but spirit as in my heart wasn't right.)

Forgiving used to be difficult for me. I believed if I forgave someone, it meant I was letting them off the hook. In reality, my forgiveness of others is for me. It's for my benefit. Father showed me that I would never experience the fullness of joy and peace He had to offer until I let go of that unforgiving spirit.

An unforgiving spirit was a dark heaviness, a virus that had been spreading through my heart and soul for decades. It occupied my thoughts. It haunted me in my dreams. It prevented me from developing meaningful friendships. I laugh every time I think about how I said more than a few times in the past that if I ran into a certain girl from high school (who was my main tormentor), I would punch her in the face. Do you think that bitterness was a driving force in my life?

I prayed about forgiving others and asked Father to help me understand how to do it. How could I just let go of all the terrible things people had done to me? I thought, *It's not fair! They should be punished!*

He clearly showed me that, as I had been holding on to all these wrongs and letting them occupy space in my mind, the people who had committed them had moved on. They weren't thinking about what they had done to me. They probably didn't even remember me. So who was I really hurting by holding on? Who was I hurting by replaying the wrongs in my head? Me, obviously. There's an old saying that a person refusing to forgive someone is like drinking a glass of poison and then waiting for the other person to die. It is only toxic to the person who refuses to forgive.

Letting go of all the offenses and the right to get even was a necessary step along my journey. No physical healing would have come without it. There was a day where hours were spent forgiving *every* person from my past who had wronged me in some way. It was a really long list! In the beginning, it was difficult to think about those people, and I would relive the traumatic moments; but as more people came to my mind, I laughed at the offenses I had been carrying. With each person I forgave, I felt freed. Not carrying those burdens anymore was a soul cleansing. I highly recommend it.

I'm guessing there are some people in your past or present you need to forgive. Be advised: Unbelievers, and even some believers, won't understand how you can do it. Some will tell you that you should not forget what someone has done, and that it's okay to remain angry. After all, you're only human. They will say you should do whatever you can to get back at them, and some may even offer suggestions about how best to achieve revenge. People offered these suggestions after learning why my seemingly perfect second marriage ended. They said I should not forgive him for what he did. They said I should tell everyone we knew my side of the story before he told them his side of the story. They couldn't understand how I wasn't just falling apart because of his betrayal, how I could consider him my friend, or how I could be so full of joy. I had let go and forgiven him. As a direct result, for the first time in my life, I had peace. My soul was at rest.

Isaiah 38:17 (NABRE) says, "Peace in place of bitterness! You have preserved my life from the pit of destruction; behind your back you cast all my sins."

Don't get me wrong, it wasn't an easy process. Everyone works through their proverbial junk differently. For me, the ability to forgive came through a process of recognizing the hurt, crying countless tears, and then letting it all go as Father took the pain from me.

Past hurtful experiences could, and would, surface at the most inconvenient times. I could be in the grocery store or at work. In many instances, I was awakened out of a deep sleep to a thought or image of a person that elicited a negative emotional response from me. I believe that was the Holy Spirit bringing to remembrance an area my unforgiving heart was still holding onto. When that thought or image came, instead of burying it (as I was prone to do in the past), I would grab a shovel and dig it up. Resurrecting old wounds was not easy, but I would spend whatever time was needed to let it go. There were times I cried for hours and even days at a stretch (which is not necessarily the best method, but it's what worked for me). These were gut-wrenching cries, sobs, and wails as I forgave and poured out all of my fears, bitterness, and pain before Him. As each tear fell, I imagined them dropping into the cupped hands of my Father.

Years later, after this whole process was complete, I found a beautiful Scripture that describes exactly what I had envisioned. Psalms 56:8 (NLT) says, "You keep track of all my sorrows. You have collected all my tears in your bottle. You have recorded each one in your book."

By envisioning each tear falling into His hands, I was able to let go of the unforgiving spirit attached to the memory that had caused them. Letting those tears go meant He was holding them, along with all the pain and heartache that came with them. I told myself that if He was holding the tears, then there was no reason for me to hold onto the trauma any longer. By leaning on His strength and surrendering to that process, I was able to supernaturally let go and watch as the strongholds in my life were torn down one at a time.

Some of you will say there's no way I could get over everything I went through without extensive psychological counseling, but I'm telling you He is the best Counselor available. With just one word from Him, He can heal what years of counseling never could heal. He can erase every emotional scar you have if you'll just cooperate with Him. Ask Him to show you any areas of an unforgiving spirit or emotional hurt that exist in your life. You won't need an audible voice from God to recognize where there is a problem. *Your negative response to a thought or an image will be a key indicator there is something you need to deal with.* Then ask Him to show you how to deal with it, and as uncomfortable as it may be, deal with it (everybody will deal with it differently).

And don't let go until you . . . well, let go.

Be assured that once you have forgiven, Satan will try to bring that old hurt back up. He'll try to convince you that you really haven't forgiven. Remember, forgiving doesn't necessarily mean you forget. Forgiving doesn't wipe that memory out of your mind like it never happened. Over time, that memory will fade. Until that time comes, however, it is your choice how you will respond to the lies of the enemy. You can either accept them or reject them. I have had many opportunities to change my mind about forgiving people from my past, but once I experienced the freedom that accompanied forgiving, I could never be persuaded by the father of lies to turn back.

I want to encourage you, for yourself, to let go. There is no past too dark or too deep that can't be healed. You can do it with His help. You are hurting no one but yourself by hanging on. Let God do a healing work in your heart like He did in mine, and experience for yourself the peace that passes all understanding.

Philippians 4:7 (NLT) says, "Then you will experience God's peace, which exceeds anything we can understand. His peace will guard your hearts and minds as you live in Christ Jesus."

Psalm 103:10–12 (MSG)

"He doesn't treat us as our sins deserve,
nor pay us back in full for our wrongs.
As high as heaven is over the earth,
so strong is his love to those who fear him.
And as far as sunrise is from sunset,
he has separated us from our sins."

CHAPTER FIVE

Why Now?

I spent the next several years growing and flourishing in my newly discovered emotional and spiritual freedom. Many people who knew me before 2007 didn't recognize me when they saw me. I was, literally, a new creation on the inside, and it was evident on the outside. I also met my second-only-to-Father guy, Patrick, during that time at church. He's a spirit-filled believer and a man after God's own heart. He is a gentleman and a warrior all rolled into one handsome package. Ladies, you know that's a deadly combination!

We had both suffered trauma in our previous marriages, and neither one of us had ever intended to marry again. When we met, we were both content in our relationships with Father and expected to remain single for the rest of our lives (which we were quite happy to do, by the way). Boy, did Father have other plans for us. We were married in 2009. We knew He had something amazing planned for us as a team. We were focused on Him together, eagerly waiting to hear what He would tell us to do next. Life couldn't have been much better.

By 2011, my thyroid condition was regulated with medication and my lab tests had all remained normal. The symptoms from the Sjögren's syndrome were tolerable, not affecting my day-to-day activities much, and I had learned to take it easy on the not-so-good days. What happened next took me completely by surprise. One morning, my right ankle was swollen and hurting to the point that putting any pressure on it was unbearable. Over the next several days, I developed a severe, itchy rash all over my body, which became most pronounced in what is called a "butterfly rash," an unmistakable rash that appears across the cheeks and bridge of the nose. I was devastated when I saw it because I knew exactly what it was: a telltale sign of lupus, which is another autoimmune disease.

My thoughts immediately turned to my oldest sister who had been diagnosed with lupus in her teen years. It had ravaged her body, and she was on dialysis for many years. She had two kidney transplants, a heart attack that required the implantation of a defibrillator, and more medications than I could comprehend. She was losing all her teeth from the anti-rejection medication she had been taking. I can't even begin to count all of the hospitalizations and treatments she went through. I had personal, firsthand knowledge of what this disease was capable of doing to the human body.

After getting confirmation that it was, in fact, lupus, I broke down and cried out to Father right there in the doctor's office. I asked Him the age-old question: *Why? Why now? Why now when I'm seeking after You with my whole heart? Father, I don't understand!*

In my mind, if the diagnosis had come when I was living in the midst of my sin, when I was far from Him, I could have understood. But why was it happening when I had totally surrendered myself to Him?

As I was lying on that cold doctor's table pleading with Father for an answer, I remember hearing His one-word response to my questions as clearly as if it were yesterday. Softly, gently, I heard the word: "Sin."

Based on my understanding at the time, I took that to mean I had allowed this disease into my body because of all of the sins I had committed in the past. I'll just say it: sin has consequences. I figured, I had sown to the flesh, and now my flesh was reaping corruption, as Galatians 6:8 says it would. You can't treat your body the way I did and not see some bad things happen as a result. You can't smoke for years and not expect to develop a cough or lung cancer. You can't overeat for years and not become overweight. Cause - and effect, sowing and reaping is a fact, and no one is exempt from that principle—whether you're a believer or an unbeliever. My logic was, I had sinned, so I'd opened the door for the devil to come in and bring lupus with him. It was my fault.

Here's the thing: *When you think something is your fault, it is very difficult to actively resist it*. Believing you're to blame for the consequences of sin, while true, can also lead to the slippery slope of condemnation. Condemnation renders you passive. In my case, in addition to believing I had brought all the sicknesses in my body on myself, the doctors had told me that the diseases were incurable, so what was the point in fighting against them?

Lying there on the doctor's table, I owned the diagnosis of lupus. My sin, my problem. Deception had its claws deep in me because there was one person that I had for-gotten to include in the process of forgiving all those years back: myself. I was living in a constant state of guilt and shame because of my life choices. Accepting forgiveness from Father was easy for me, forgiving others had been easy (with His help), but forgiving myself—not so much. In a way, I was viewing the sickness and disease in my body as penance for my sins. So if I got better, I got better. If not, I would just live with it because it was my fault anyway.

I see now how wrong my interpretation of His one-word answer had been and how it kept me from receiving my healing for many years. When I asked Father "Why?" and He answered, "Sin," He meant the sin that was ushered into the world with the fall of Adam in the garden. Adam's sin allowed sickness, disease, death, and all manner of evil to become a part of our world. *This is a major distinction to understand.*

God's Word says that His mercies are new every morn-ing (Lamentations 3:22–23) and that for the one who believes on Him the blood of the Lamb covers *all* our sins—past, present, and future (Hebrews 10:10–12 NLT). By taking responsibility for my sins in the form of sickness in my body, by owning them, *I was denying the finished work of the cross.* I was denying Jesus' death, burial, and resurrection. I was saying that His blood wasn't enough to cover what I had done.

Think about that for a minute. This is a really big deal, and it's a prevalent mindset among Christians. This mind-set is bondage and is in total cooperation with the enemy's plan for our lives. We don't have to cooperate though. We

Sin · ushered in @ the Fall

can choose to believe the truth and reject the lie. The truth is, other than denying Him, there is *no sin* that is beyond the grace of God. Yes, sin has consequences, but there is *nothing* that is beyond the reach of the cross. Nothing. Nada. Zilch. And just as the one man, Adam, ushered sin into the world, Jesus became sin and took the judgment from our heavenly Father for us (2 Corinthians 5:21). He handled all of that mess, so there's no reason for us to have to live with any of it.

But, at the time, despite knowing deep in my heart that my Father loved me and didn't want me to stay in that place of sickness, I just didn't know how to get out. Over the next year I was diagnosed with degenerative disk disease in my back, a bulged disk in my lower back that would incapacitate me for weeks at a time, and carpal tunnel syndrome in my right wrist. The carpal tunnel caused numbness and tingling in my hand and fingers, as well as pain, and I had to wear a brace to bed every night to prevent those symptoms from keeping me up.

I was a court reporter at the time (the career I pursued after sickness forced me out of nursing), and carpal tunnel was considered "normal," so I wasn't surprised when I was diagnosed with it. In fact, when I first started school to become a court reporter, I was informed that court reporters get carpal tunnel and that's just the way it is.

Just as it's difficult to resist something you think is your fault, it's equally as hard to resist something you're expecting.

If you're expecting something, in your mind you've already envisioned it happening and prepared yourself for it. You've accepted it as the definitive outcome, as something

Sjögrens Syndrom
Lupus
Degenerative Disk Diseas
Bulged Disk
Carpal Tunnel

that can't be changed. So when it does happen, you accept it.

A few common examples of this way of thinking as it pertains to aging include:

- "When you turn forty years old, you'll start falling apart."
- "It's normal for your joints to ache when you get older."
- "It's normal for your memory to get bad in old age."

Do any of those supposed "facts" sound familiar? Maybe you've used these phrases without thinking about it. The bottom line is, what you expect will happen. It may not happen immediately, but it will happen certainly.

All the while I was speaking out 1 Peter 2:24, "By His stripes I'm healed," and wondering not only why I wasn't getting better but why the conditions were getting worse.

I lived with the frustration of knowing the Word, believing the Word, speaking the Word, and not seeing any change for many years before Father called me to go to Charis Bible College (Charis) in August 2013. It was there that I got the teaching and direction I needed. Through what I learned at Charis, I received a revelation of healing, which led to the complete healing of my body in March 2014.

With 100 percent certainty, I can say that without the teaching and instruction I received at Charis, I would still be in the same position I was in for all those years: a believer who was unable to access the healing Jesus died for me to have (which is part of my salvation) over two thousand years ago. The Charis curriculum taught me that healing is not an add-on to salvation.

Healing is as much mine—right now—as is my forgiven sin.

Now it's your turn to know what I know.

What you expect, WILL HAPPEN

Romans 12:2 (NKJV)

"And do not be conformed to this world,
but be transformed by the renewing of your
mind, that you may prove what is that good
and acceptable and perfect will of God."

CHAPTER SIX

The Victory Key

Spoiler alert!

This is it. This chapter reveals the key to my receiving healing. Without that key, I would still be stuck in a body that was dying a little more every day.

The key is revelation.

A lack of revelation is why, for years, I quoted the Scriptures and nothing happened. A lack of revelation left me disappointed in my beliefs, left me sick and hurting, left me questioning the ability of my God, and left me questioning His willingness to heal me and my worthiness to receive His healing.

A lack of revelation left me believing that I was waiting on God to heal me, when in fact, He had healed me two thousand years ago on the cross and was waiting for me to receive it.

My first term of Bible college started in August 2013. Because of my upbringing in the Word, and the previous six years spent actively pursuing the heart of the Father, I believed I had a strong grasp on the Word. You could ask me for a Scripture that related to anything and I could quote it. Do you need money? Here you go: Philippians 4:19 (NKJV) says, "My God will supply all your need according to His riches in glory." Do you need healing? This one is on a loop in my head: 1 Peter 2:24 (KJV) says by His stripes you were healed.

Through the teachings, however, I learned that there is a big difference between head knowledge and revelation knowledge.

I began to hear about this "revelation" word in the first few weeks of school. Everywhere I turned I heard, "I got a revelation of this" and "I got a revelation of that." First of all, I didn't even really know what revelation was in practical terms. "Getting a revelation" seemed very spiritual and deep and, quite frankly, way out of my reach. I had certainly never personally experienced it. What does it even mean to "have a revelation"? When I asked people, their responses included, "I don't know how I know; I just know." Or "A light bulb went on and I get it now." Or, my favorite one, "I just know that I know that I know it in my knower." I wanted to scream, "What do you know, and what is a 'knower'?!"

With all due respect to those well-meaning people, those responses weren't helpful. The irony, of course, is that since I've had a revelation of my own, my definition isn't much better. I describe it as the Word coming alive—not just *for* you, but *in* you. It's the Word becoming yours, and becoming so real to you that nothing can convince you otherwise. It's knowing that it doesn't matter what anyone tells you, what the doctors tell you, what your lab reports say, or even what your body tells you, because you know the truth, and you will not be moved.

Imagine you are standing on the edge of the Grand

Canyon with your toes dangling precariously over the edge. Go ahead. Picture it. Outstretched before you to the other side is a tightrope. That tightrope is whatever it is that you are facing right now—cancer, lupus, arthritis, injury, emotional trauma, bankruptcy, etc. Now, unless you're a professional tightrope walker, you would more than likely be terrified to step out onto that rope. You might make it one or two steps, but as soon as the wind blew or the rope shifted the tiniest bit, as soon as that symptom came or as soon as that negative lab report came back, you would lose your balance and fall. Now imagine another rope right above you that is also stretched across the canyon. Attached to that rope is a harness that has been securely fastened around you. You test the rope and the harness, and they are secure and sure to hold you. There is no doubt in your mind that you can cross the tightrope without falling because you have the harness as security. You will make it to the other side. You can confidently step out onto that rope and no matter what comes, you know that you are going to the other side.

Revelation is the harness that produces unwavering confi- *dence and faith in the face of any circumstance.*

Each person may have a different definition of what revelation is to them, but one thing is certain: when you get one, you know it, and everything will change when you do.

Ironically, my first revelation was that I had no revelation of my own. Looking back, it was clear that my entire

Christian walk had been spent living on the revelation of others. In their revelations is where I was searching for my own healing. I went to conferences on healing, hoping to hear about some new method I hadn't tried yet or some secret ingredient I was missing that would get God to move on my behalf. My faith was in people with the gift of healing prayer for me, hoping *they* would have the revelation needed to get me healed. If I knew someone who had gotten healed, my plan was to emulate what they did—read this book, pray for an hour a day, quote this Scripture ten times a day, fast once a month—but none of that was working for me.

Although I wasn't doing it consciously, my actions were all performance-based, a crazy circus act I was putting on for God. You know, old habits.

Healing—rather than a relationship with my Father—was my objective. That was a major point. Don't miss it. Here it is again for the folks in the back:

Healing—rather than a relationship with my Father—was my objective.

I was seeking first my healing because that's what I thought I needed the most. It is a fact that I needed the personal benefits that came from serving the Lord (which includes healing), but I had been wasting time and effort because I had failed to invest time into getting to *know* Him. Rather than trying to bootleg my healing off someone who'd gotten a revelation about it, I should have been looking into His Word to get a revelation of my own. After all, if God communicated through His Word directly to others, He would communicate through His Word directly to me too.

But, because I didn't know that then, I was looking for a formula, a step-by-step instruction guide on how to get healed. I wanted A + B + C = healing. For example, one of my formulas (I'm not making this up!) was to quote 1 Peter 2:24 ten times a day, fast once a month, and read the same book a person who got healed had read. I thought if I followed that formula, I might receive my healing. I was trying so hard!

By the time I reached Bible college, however, formulas were not equaling healing. I was accepting whatever came to me and dealing with it.

Like many of you, I was tired of believing and not receiving. It was easier to just accept the pain and disease than to keep believing. I was obviously missing something, and I had no idea what it was, so I wondered why I should keep trying to figure it out. I had believed and experienced disappointment one too many times. My faith in God's Word was shaken, and unbelief was waging war in my soul and winning.

A word on unbelief: Unbelief can be caused by many things—lack of teaching, wrong teaching, or your physical senses, just to name a few—and it can walk side by side with faith. We see the simultaneous presence of faith and unbelief demonstrated several times in Scripture. Mark 9:23–24 (NKJV) says, "Help my unbelief!" This was belief and unbelief rolled up into one package.

Scripture also reveals that unbelief can make faith of

no effect. James 1:6–7 (KJV) is a perfect example: "But let him ask in faith, nothing wavering. For he that wavereth is like a wave of the sea driven with the wind and tossed. For let not that man think that he shall receive any thing of the Lord." If you have faith and waver (unbelief), you won't get what you are believing for.

The good news is that Matthew 21:21 (KJV) says, "Jesus answered and said unto them, Verily I say unto you, If ye have faith, and doubt not, ye shall not only do this which is done to the fig tree, but also if ye shall say unto this mountain, Be thou removed, and be those cast into the sea; it shall be done." If you have faith and don't doubt (unbelief), you can move *any* mountain. (I'll show you later how to get rid of your doubt, regardless of your circumstances.)

Back to revelation. Here's one for you: Your born-again spirit *already has* all the revelation you need to live victoriously in every area of your life. Now, if you're not born again, let's fix that first. Romans 10:9 (NKJV) says, "That if you confess with your mouth the Lord Jesus and believe in your heart that God has raised Him from the dead, you will be saved." That's all there is to being born again: speaking and believing. No hoops to jump through. No pomp. No circumstance. No drama. So, if you want access to *all* God has for you, just say this out loud:

Jesus, I've kept You out of my life for too long. I know that I'm a sinner and that I can't save myself. By faith, I receive Your gift of salvation. I am ready to trust You as my Lord and Savior. I believe You are the Son of God Who died on the cross for my sins and rose from the dead on the third day. Thank You for bearing my sins and giving me the gift of eternal life. Come into my heart, Jesus, and be my Savior. Amen.

For those of you who just prayed that prayer of salvation, congratulations and welcome to the family. Your salvation is a free gift and part of the reason Jesus died for you.

Operative words here: part of the reason. Saving you from an eternity in hell is one of many free gifts of Jesus' atonement. Sadly, most Christians forfeit receiving all the other free gifts He died for us to have because of ignorance. We do indeed perish for lack of knowledge.

So let's not keep perishing, shall we? Back to that revelation: For those who are born again, you *already have* the revelation you need for healing, freedom, prosperity, etc. God's Word tells you that when you were born again, He put Jesus' Spirit into your heart, that your spirit is one with Jesus' Spirit, and that as Jesus' Spirit is, so are you *right now* (Galatians 4:6: 1 Corinthians 6:17: 1 John 4:17). This means your spirit, *right now*, is complete, healed, whole, and knows what Jesus knows. God wouldn't promise you things in the Word and then not equip you to receive them. You have what it takes to receive right now—*today*.

The key is in getting that revelation you have in your born-again spirit into your soul, which is your mind, your will, and your emotions. See, unlike your spirit that becomes brand new and perfect immediately upon accepting Christ, your soul requires some work to get it in line with God's Word. But, once your spirit and your soul are in agreement, your body will follow.

Your mind is like the valve between your spirit and your

What + who you ARE IN the Spirit has to go through your soul
MIND - WILL + EMOTIONS

body. If your mind is closed off to the things of God, what's in your spirit can't flow into your body. *You open that valve up by renewing your mind to God's Word,* and it is in the renewing of your mind that transformation will take place in your body (Romans 12:2). Isn't it good to know you're not waiting on God for revelation and He's not withholding it from you? I can't tell you how many times I have said in the past, "I'm waiting for God to give me a revelation about healing, and then I'll be able to receive." Baloney! I wasn't waiting on Him; He was waiting on me.

The same is true for you. You already have whatever you lack in the natural on the inside of you, and you just need to learn how to draw it out.

With God's help, I'll be your how-to teacher.

Romans 8:16 (KJV)

"The Spirit itself beareth witness with our
spirit,
that we are the children of God."
. . . that we are victorious!
. . . that we are prosperous!
. . . and that we are healed!

CHAPTER SEVEN

Let's Do This

There are four practical principles you can begin applying to your life today. (Are you noticing a right-now theme with receiving from God? It doesn't have to take a long time. You can receive as quickly as you renew your mind to His truths.) I guarantee they will open you up to start receiving revelation about the Word. As I applied these very principles to my life, Father started taking me to Scriptures that I just knew were written for *me*, Scriptures that would heal *me* when planted and nurtured in my spirit. He started teaching me about who I am in Christ and what that means to me in my everyday walk. He taught me about the power and authority I have here on earth because of the sacrifice of His Son. Once I started receiving understanding and those truths began to penetrate from my spirit to my soul (mind, will, and emotions), my healing became inevitable. The same will happen for you.

The first of those four practical principles is to remove *1.* distractions. I believe distractions are the number one hindrances to receiving revelation. I like to refer to them as the devil's *weapons of mass distraction*. In his book *Dangerous Wonder*, Michael Yaconelli said, "We did not want to stop

1. Remove Distractions

hearing God's voice. Indeed, God kept on speaking. But our lives became louder. The increasing crescendo of our possessions, the ear-piercing noise of busyness, and the soul-smothering volume of our endless activity drowned out the still, small voice of God."[1]

You must stop, take a breath, get alone, and spend some time in the presence of Father and in the presence of His Word. I am not condemning you, but I am challenging you to evaluate your priorities. What do you do with the majority of your free time? Is it consumed with social media, television, or movies? Those things in themselves are not bad, but I am challenging you to deny whatever it is that competes for your attention and instead dedicate that time to Him. It doesn't matter if it's for ten minutes or three hours (although, revelation is a function of quality *and* quantity time in the Word). It doesn't matter if you read the Word, pray, or just sit in silence during that time. If you are constantly on the go, always thinking about what's next on the to-do list (I was the queen of the to-do list), or if you always have some noise plugged into your ears, you will miss that still, small voice.

The second practical principle is to ask. Simply ask Father for wisdom and revelation. For the longest time, I just didn't think to do that, but James 1:5 clearly tells you that if you lack wisdom you can ask Him for it. Not only will He give it to you *liberally*, but He won't make fun of you for asking. Have you ever asked someone a question and gotten the "Are you stupid?" look in response? That won't happen with God. He *wants* you to seek His understanding. He *wants* the answers you are seeking to be

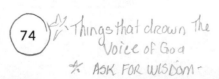

Things that drown the Voice of God
ASK FOR WISDOM

revealed to your soul. You may have to ask a lot of questions, but go ahead—God's got an inexhaustible supply of wisdom and revelation. You can't wear Him out.

Paul prayed a prayer for the Ephesians asking for this very thing, so I took that prayer from Ephesians 1:17–19 and made it my own. My prayer went something like this:

> Father, give me the Spirit of wisdom and revelation in the knowledge of You. I pray that the eyes of my understanding are being enlightened and my heart is being flooded with light so I can understand the hope to which You have called me, the riches of Your glorious inheritance in me, and what is the exceeding greatness of Your power toward me because I believe.

As I prayed that prayer, as I renewed my mind to His Word and spoke it into my life, a confidence sprang up that revelation was coming. As that Scripture took root in my heart, I noticed that the words I was praying began to change.

Instead of praying, *Father, give me* a Spirit of wisdom and revelation, I was saying, *Father, thank you* for giving me a Spirit of wisdom and revelation.

Instead of praying, *I pray that* the eyes of my understanding are being enlightened and my heart is being flooded with light, I was praying, *Thank you that* the eyes of my understanding *are* enlightened and that my heart *is* flooded with Your light!

I started *expecting* those things in my spirit man to be

ASK ALOT of Q's

PRaying Eph

revealed to my mind. Expectation. We have talked about negative expectation. I was expecting carpal tunnel because most court reporters get it. I was expecting lupus because my sister had it and there was a history of autoimmune diseases on my mom's side of the family. As I prayed this prayer, the power of positive expectation started working in my favor. I was expecting revelation. I was expecting understanding.

I remember getting to the place many times where I felt like "it" was just right there, like I was on the verge of understanding something amazing. It was the feeling of being suspended weightless in midair right before a big fall. It was anticipation and excitement. My spirit would be jumping on the inside of me so much so that I could feel it—like a constant quivering. I think my spirit was excited that my mind was finally getting it! Typically, very shortly after experiencing that anticipatory state, I would have some big breakthrough in my mind.

I prayed that prayer from Ephesians at the beginning of every alone-time I had with Father, and then I implemented the third practical principle: praying in the Spirit.

3. Praying in the Spirit (also known as praying in your prayer language, praying in tongues, or speaking in tongues) is a critical key to receiving revelation knowledge from God. First Corinthians 14:2 (NKJV) says, "For he that speaks in a tongue does not speak to men but to God, for no one understands him; however, in the spirit he speaks mysteries." This means that when we pray in the Spirit, our natural mind doesn't understand what we're saying (1 Corinthians 14:14)—nor does anyone else for that

matter—but Father does. Praying in the Spirit is our direct line of communication with Him.

So, you might ask if your mind doesn't understand, how does that lead to revelation? Good question. Paul seemed to have the answer. Paul says a few times in Scripture that he was teaching the mysteries of God, and he clearly states that he received revelation of those mysteries from the Holy Spirit (1 Corinthians 2:10).

I believe the answer to the "how" question is this: 1 Corinthians 14:13 (KJV) says, "Wherefore let him that speaketh in an unknown tongue pray that he may interpret." Paul instructed those he taught to pray for an interpretation of their prayer language. I think it's fair to assume he was practicing what he preached in that area, and that resulted in revelation knowledge of the mysteries of God.

What this looks like in your everyday life is this: You have to choose between option A and option B. Both are good options, but you want what's best. So ask Father to give you wisdom in making the decision, and spend some time praying in the Spirit. As you pray with those options in mind, I guarantee you that it will become clear to you which one is the right choice for you. You will have peace with one over the other. I've done this many times with problems I've faced. Here's my approach:

- Ask for wisdom.
- Pray in the Spirit.
- Ask God for the interpretation of what I'd just prayed.

Almost without exception, I receive the answer. As

you pray in tongues, that wisdom you've been asking for according to James 1:5 comes. That "thing" that you're seeking breakthrough on actually breaks through. Revelation comes.

I firmly believe this happens as you spend time praying in the Spirit, and I have personally experienced it (more on that soon).

Along with creating an environment to receive revelation, there are many other benefits to praying in the Spirit. One of those benefits being that as you pray, you can be assured you're praying the perfect prayer because it is not coming from your natural understanding; it is coming directly from your spirit man (which is perfect and identical to Jesus' Spirit) and going directly to the heart of God.

Your spirit knows what you need to pray, even when you don't have the words. You know those times where you go in to pray and sit there in silence because you have no idea what to say, then you get up and go do something else because the silence is uncomfortable and you feel like it's not doing a thing for you anyway? Well, those are the perfect times to just let your spirit take the wheel and pray for you. Your spirit will intercede for you when you don't know what—or how—to pray.

The Word tells us that the Spirit bears witness with our spirits. The first time I heard that Scripture, all I could think was, Huh? Romans 8:16 (NKJV) says, "The Spirit Himself bears witness with our spirit that we are children of God." To "bear witness" means to corroborate, confirm, prove, or to testify to.[2] I used to read that Scripture as "bears witness to our spirit." Read that way, it said to me that the Holy

Spirit was telling my spirit things my spirit didn't know, that my spirit was missing something. However, if you look closely at that Scripture, one word changes the whole meaning. The Spirit bears witness *with* my spirit, not *to* it.

In order to bear witness *with* someone, both sides have to be in agreement and of the same understanding. If you're going to bear witness with someone in a court of law, you're going to testify to the exact same thing they testify to. Your stories will be the same. Likewise, the Spirit joins *with* your spirit to testify to your *soul* that you are a child of God, that you are healed and that you are free. *In turn, as your mind begins to bear witness with your own spirit, transformation will take place in your body.* This is the opening of the valve we described in the previous chapter.

I believe praying in tongues is a vital component in the process of receiving revelation, and each of the practical principles we've discussed so far is important to incorporate in your everyday life. But I believe the fourth one is the most crucial: you have to keep God's Word in the forefront of your mind.

The more attention you give to God's Word, the less time your mind has to focus on anything else. You have to look to His Word before you look to anything else. You have to believe His Word before you believe the voice of another. You can't expect the Word to become alive in you if you say a quick prayer in the morning and then spend the rest of the day taking inventory of what is still wrong in your body or meditating on the bad doctor's report. If you received a bad doctor's report, the very next response should be, "What does the Word of God say about that?"

Every time that report wants to come back into your mind or that symptom into your body, shut it down with what the Word says about it (and the Word has *a lot* to say about bad reports—whether they be physical, financial, emotional, mental, etc.). If you have to counter that negative thought with His Word a hundred times a day, do it.

Consistency is the key to seeing results as you apply these four principles to your life on a daily basis. Consistently applying them is how your mind will be renewed and align/agree with your spirit man. I know this is true because it's what the Word says.

The Word instructs us on the need for consistency in order to receive understanding. Second Timothy 2:7 (NKJV) says, "Consider what I say, and may the Lord give you understanding in all things." That word "consider" implies much more than a casual glance at His Word. It means to think about or ponder. It means to meditate on. When I say meditate, I don't mean sitting cross-legged on the floor, palms up, and chanting an incantation. Meditation means filling your mind (flooding and saturating it) with His Word. This takes time, effort, and study, but the promise is clear: if you consider what He says, you *will* receive understanding.

I love the *Strong's Concordance* definition of the word *understanding* in this verse. It means a "running together" or a "flowing together with."[3] In other words, a connecting of the dots. Praise God! As you consider the words He speaks, the dots will be connected between your mind and your spirit and revelation *will* come.

You may be saying to yourself that you already do all

those things and it's still not working for you. If that's you, I challenge you to really take a look at yourself and be honest. If you had asked me before I'd received my revelation of healing if I was doing those things, I would have emphatically said yes too. But when I look back and I'm honest about it, I wasn't applying those principles with any consistency to be able to see any results. I can tell you from experience that if you will consistently apply those four principles—removing distractions, asking for wisdom and revelation, praying in the Spirit, and keeping the Word in the forefront of your mind—you will get your own revelation, and that revelation will change your life.

Numbers 23:19 (NKJV)

"God is not a man, that He should lie,
Nor a son of man, that He should repent.
Has He said, and will He not do?
Or has He spoken, and will He not make it
good?"

CHAPTER EIGHT

What Is a Promise?

While I diligently applied those four principles to my everyday life, Father revealed a few barriers that were standing in the way of my receiving His healing. These barriers had to be removed, and I believe they are common to many believers who aren't experiencing healing in their bodies today. Identifying and recognizing these barriers in your own life early on will lead to you receiving your healing that much quicker. Most of the barriers revealed were related to wrong mindsets.

According to *Merriam-Webster's Dictionary*, the definition of *mindset* includes "a particular way of thinking" or a "fixed state of mind."[1] We all have specific mindsets that are shaped by any number of things as we move through life, such as what we're taught in school and church, how we're raised (i.e., if we experienced a loving home, an abusive home, a strict home, etc.), and how we're treated by others, just to name a few. These life experiences cause us to view situations in ways that are unique to us. A classic example of this would be the glass-half-full versus the glass-half-empty mentality. The same physical element exists—a glass with water in it—but two people will describe that same glass

CRYSTAL –

in a completely different way based on the way they think. Personal life experiences play a big role in establishing our mindsets and directly shape our personal views about God, as well as how we interpret His written and spoken Word. So much so that I believe at times we examine God's Word in the light of our experiences rather than rightly examining our experiences in the light of God's Word. This in turn affects how we will be able to receive from Him.

Whether we recognize it or not, we all have a personalized set of glasses through which we see the world. Some see through rose-colored glasses, some through blue-tinted glasses, and others through very dark glasses. All shades will alter and distort what you see. Everything in the world isn't actually pink, but that's the way it appears looking through rose-colored glasses. Everything in the world isn't dark and ominous, but that's the way it appears looking through very dark glasses, and so on. Evaluating your world based on what you're seeing through those colored glasses is the same as examining God's Word through the tinted glasses of your life experiences. You are looking at God's Word through the reality of what you're going through and seeing how God's Word holds up.

We need to take off those tinted glasses and hold up the magnifying glass of the Word of God to take a really close look at the circumstance. Not only will the distortion caused by the tinted glasses be removed, but the magnifying glass will make everything crystal clear. You see the good and you see the bad. If we examine the world filtered through the magnifying glass of the Word of God instead of through the distortion of tinted glasses, we will see the truth about every situation that is placed before us.

So why do we choose to look through tinted glasses? Maybe it's just because we aren't aware we're doing it, but I believe it's most likely because we just can't make sense of the situation any other way. We try to explain away something that is happening in our lives by forcing God's Word or His character to fit into the situation. That may mean taking His Word out of context or twisting the truth to make it fit in with what we're experiencing. A "good Christian"—especially one who reads the Word—wouldn't do that, would they?

Well, this good Christian did without even realizing it, and my point of view was a hindrance to receiving my healing because it gave me a skewed image of Father.

Let me explain. My oldest sister, Jacquelyn, was killed in a car accident in 2003. As I mentioned before, she had been diagnosed with lupus at a very young age, and it had destroyed her body. Physically, she was a train wreck; emotionally, she was miserable. After she died, I reasoned that God knew her condition and that, because He is so merciful and good, He took her home.

That explanation sounded good—and may even sound good and reasonable to some of you if you'll admit it—but most importantly, it put my heart at ease. It made her death easier to swallow. The thought that my merciful Father had put her out of her misery was of comfort to me.

The devil is very good at making lies easy to swallow.

After all, that logic made complete sense to me: God is good. He didn't want her to suffer. So He took her home. But it wasn't true. Father did *not* take my sister. His plan for her life was better than anyone could have ever imagined. His plan for her was complete healing and restoration of her body. That's what His Word says. My Father. Did. Not. Take. Her. That was the work of Satan.

In my mind, I was holding God's Word up to the light of her death by picking and choosing Scriptures about His mercy and His great love for us that fit in nicely with that experience. What I should have been doing was exposing the devil by holding her death up to the light of God's Word. If I had looked beyond that particular way of thinking and beyond what my heart wanted to believe, the Bible clearly would have told me that it's the devil who comes for three purposes—to steal, to kill, and to destroy—and that it's God Who comes to bring life (John 10:10).

Thinking that Father took Jacquelyn's life out of His goodness, or that He was allowing sickness to stay in my body as a consequence of my sin, was a direct assault on His true nature. Would a good Father take the life of His sick child in order to end their suffering, or would He much rather see them healed so they could live a long life and be a testimony to others? Would a good Father allow His child to remain sick to teach them something, or would He long to see them well so they could tell of His goodness in the land of the living?

It would be hard to love Father completely and to confidently receive *anything* from Him when we wrongly assign Him characteristics that are based solely on our experiences.

I have found that changing a mindset is sometimes as simple as recognizing that the one you have is wrong.

When I realized Father didn't take my sister and that my thinking had been wrong, I had an "Aha!" moment, and my mindset changed instantly. Then I got angry. I got angry at the devil for stealing her life. I got angry at myself that, in my ignorance, I had placed her death on my Father, the giver of life, the One Who sent His Son that she might live. His Word says His thoughts toward us are *only* good, *only* pure, and *only* lovely, and that He is *only* good, *all* the time. He can be no other way, and that is the light under which I now choose to view every life situation. My mindset has changed—permanently.

I can tell you with certainty that, because of that change in my view of Father, I know that it is His will to heal all people and every disease. I am passionate on this point, and I would challenge anyone who doesn't believe 100 percent that He heals all people and every disease to find one instance in the New Testament where Jesus withheld healing from anyone, or where He said, "Sorry. You haven't learned your lesson yet. You need to stay sick a little longer." That would be outside of the nature of our Father, and I won't waver on that fact based on an experience where the opposite has occurred.

I have prayed for people, believed, and felt the healing power of Jesus sweep through their bodies, and they still died. Why? I don't know. I may never know until I see Jesus face to face, but that won't stop me from praying for the next person. There are many reasons why people don't receive their healing, but I know beyond a shadow of a doubt that one of those reasons is not because God is withholding it.

Over time, Father revealed several other ways I was allowing wrong thinking to hinder my relationship with Him, and they are especially prevalent in those who have been believing for healing for an extended period of time.

In one passage of Scripture, Romans 4:17–21, God showed me two mindsets I was missing. By the way, if you are looking for a "formula" to receive healing, I believe these Scriptures are as close to it as you can get. I guarantee that if you apply the four practical principles of revelation I've shared to these Scriptures—and practice them consistently in your everyday life—they *will* work in your life and you *will* see results. I can definitively make this guarantee because it worked for me.

Let's look at the passage:

> (As it is written, I have made thee a father of many nations,) before him whom he believed, even God, who quickeneth the dead, and calleth those things which be not as though they were.
>
> Who against hope believed in hope, that he might become the father of many nations, according to that which was spoken, So shall thy seed be.
>
> And being not weak in faith, he considered not his own body now dead, when he was about an hundred years old, neither yet the deadness of Sarah's womb:
>
> He staggered not at the promise of God through unbelief; but was strong in faith, giving glory to God;

And being fully persuaded that, what he
had promised, he was able also to perform.
(KJV)

You can see in this passage that there is reference to both
hope and faith. Hope and faith are two different things.
Hope is an expectation that something good is going to
happen. Faith is knowing that it's already done. Hope is
the precursor to faith. First, Abraham had an expectation,
a hope, of something good; and then his hope turned into
faith.

The basis of his *hope* was God's promise—mindset
number 1. The basis of his *faith* is mindset number 2 (discussed in the following chapter). *pg 95*

Mindset 1: In verses 17 and 18, we see that Abraham
had hope based on God's spoken word to him. In verse 20,
that spoken word is referred to as God's promise. I believe
his hope sprang up because he had a true understanding, a
proper mindset, of what a promise coming from the mouth
of God meant. Against all odds, Abraham believed God
because God promised him that he would have a child and
that, through his child, he would be the father of many
nations. In the natural, he and Sarah were way too old to
have children. In fact, when God spoke these words to
him, Abraham was seventy-five years old (Genesis 12:4).
Can you even imagine God telling you at that age that you
would be having a child? I probably would have laughed
out loud like Sarah did! Or maybe cried. I'm not sure which
I would have done.

Unlike Abraham, I couldn't quite grasp the concept of
what a promise meant to God, so I started thinking first

about something I could wrap my head around: what a promise meant to me. If I give my word to someone that I'll do something, I will do everything I can in my power to make sure I fulfill that promise. I stand by my word. I realized that if I, as a mere human being, hold a promise I give in such high regard, how much more so will God uphold His word to me? He even says in Psalm 138:2 that He magnifies His word above all His Name. The power of His name is immeasurable, so imagine the power of His word magnified above it.

Have you ever really thought about what His promise means? When I tell you there is a promise of healing for you in the Word, how significant is that to you? Pause and think about that for a second. In this day and age where the word *promise* is overused and undervalued, a man's word doesn't hold the same weight it once held. If you have been on this earth for any length of time, you have likely been promised many things by many people. It's also probably safe to say many of those people have failed to fulfill their promises to you, leaving you hurt and disappointed. We've all been there. But again, let's not let our life experiences with people skew our concept of what a promise actually is and what it means to our Father—remove the tinted glasses, get the magnifying glass, and look again.

One of the Scriptures I meditated on to get rid of some past-experience garbage, and to change my thinking, was Numbers 23:19 (NKJV). It says:

> God is not a man, that He should lie, nor a son
> of man, that He should repent. Has He said,

and will He not do? Or has He spoken, and
will He not make it good?

I had to get it in my head that God is not a man like
the men and women in my life who had spoken promises
and broken them. God is not a mere man. In fact, God is
not a man at all. He is God. He cannot lie. It's not that He's
incapable of fibbing. It's that whatever He says is what's so.
If He called me a giraffe, I would immediately become a
giraffe. He's God.

That is why His word to us is so powerful, and we can
put the full weight of our expectations on it. I had to put
aside my experiences and convince myself that if He said it,
He's already done it through the finished works of Jesus. It
is His word. It is His bond. Not only that, but if He said it
once, even if it was two thousand years ago, I can have faith
that it still holds true and applies to me today. Hebrews
13:8 (NKJV) says, "Jesus Christ is the same yesterday, today,
and forever," and James 1:17 (KJV) says that in Him there
"is no variableness, neither shadow of turning." He is the
same and He will not change. I just had to believe and so-
lidify in my mind that infallible truth.

As I meditated on Numbers 23:19, Father began to
impress on me in a very personal way that His Word is
His promise to me. It is His covenant with me. So, when
I read in 1 Peter 2:24 that by the stripes of His Son I was
healed—a Scripture that refers to healing in the past tense,
meaning it happened a long time ago—I took that as His
direct promise to me. I put my name in the verse and began
to envision Him speaking those words to me. Teresa, by the

stripes of my Son, you were healed over two thousand years ago! I began to know—wait for it . . . in "my knower"— that those words were for me. I could believe them, I could rely on them, and I could stand on them in the face of op-

pivital

position from my body. Even though the symptoms were still present in my body, the meaning of His promise was growing stronger and the effect of the symptoms on my mind was weakening. His Words weighed more in my life than they ever had. Psalm 119:89 (NKJV) says, "Forever, O Lord, Your word is settled in heaven." His Word is settled, His Word is His promise, which means His promises are also settled in heaven.

You may be thinking, I already know about His promises. But, just stop and really examine your thinking here. Be honest and ask yourself these questions: Do I really believe God's promises are mine? Do I really believe He is speaking those promises to me? Do I really believe that if I was the only person on this earth that He still would have promised them to me?

Be honest. . .

If you dare to ask yourself those questions and answer truthfully, you may be surprised at your answers. I know I was. Your interpretation of the word *promise* is foundational in putting faith and having confidence in Father's words to you, so spend some time on this until what His promises actually mean to you are firmly settled in your heart and mind.

When I gave His promises the weight they deserved, it changed everything for me. The Word became more than just ink on a page or words in a book. I began to value each Scripture, to see it as my own, and it became alive in me.

Not only were His words forever settled in heaven, but they were becoming forever settled in my heart and in my mind.

His words are mine *because I am* His.

Romans 4:19–21 (NKJV)

"And not being weak in faith, he did not
consider his own body, already dead
(since he was about a hundred years old),
and the deadness of Sarah's womb.
He did not waver at the promise of God
through unbelief, but was strengthened in
faith, giving glory to God, and being fully
convinced that what He had promised
He was also able to perform."

CHAPTER NINE

The Beginning of Faith

We just saw in Romans 4:17–18 that Abraham's hope came from his understanding of what a promise from God meant. He had hope in that promise, and his hope in that promise led to strong, unwavering faith. I had hope because I was beginning to understand what a promise from my Father meant, and I had faith (maybe not in action yet, but I had faith). I had to come clean with myself though. The truth was, because I hadn't seen healing in my body for so many years, I had unbelief festering in my *Bingo* heart. A lack of faith wasn't my problem—it's not yours either. Unbelief was my problem, it's and what's stopping you too.

I used to get hung up on believing I didn't have enough faith. I said things like, "I must not have enough faith to receive my healing." I believe the "having enough faith" issue is a major sticking point with respect to people receiving their healing. Let me just bless you right now and put your mind at ease.

If you have been taught that you don't have enough faith, you've believed a lie.

Yes, you have to have faith to receive, but if the devil can keep you fixated on figuring out how to get more of what you already have enough of—faith—he can keep you from concentrating on the true problem: the unbelief that counters faith.

Let's examine faith. The King James Version of Romans 12:3 says, "For I say, through the grace given unto me, to every man that is among you, not to think of himself more highly than he ought to think; but to think soberly, according as God hath dealt to every man the measure of faith." Many other translations say "*a* measure of faith," but the King James translation says "*the* measure of faith" (emphasis mine).

What a difference one word makes.

Some people contend that neither "the" nor "a" were in the original text. The semantics are irrelevant because Romans 2:11 says God is no respecter of persons. If that Scripture is true (and it is), God wouldn't give some a thimble full of faith and give others a barrel full. I also don't believe Father would make promises that have to be received by faith but not equip us with enough faith to receive them. That's not how God works. He's a just God. He doesn't set us up to lose. He's all about the win. Not convinced? Okay, try this one on. Peter said you—as a believer—have "like precious faith" (2 Peter 1:1), and he had enough faith to raise Dorcas from the dead (Acts 9:36–42).

You have raise-the-dead faith *right now*.

Paul goes on to say in Galatians 2:20 that he lives by *the* faith *of* the Son of God. Since we all have been given the same measure of faith, you also have *the* faith *of* the Son of God. I don't know about you, but I'm just fine with working off of Jesus' faith! When I understood I already had the faith I needed to get healed—and that I didn't have to work for it—it took a lot of pressure off. I already had it in me, and you already have it in you.

The measure of faith is given to every born-again believer as a part of the atonement. It's another free gift (God's the most generous giver ever). So I had strong faith—the same faith Paul, Peter, and even Jesus had—but I also had unbelief, which, as I explained before, was negating my faith. The unbelief made me question—whether I wanted to admit it or not—the validity and power of His Word to work in my body. I thought, *This Word is supposed to be a living and active book, sharper than any two-edged sword, and it says I'm healed. So why isn't it working?*

I had a decision to make and a mindset to change. I was either going to believe every bit of His Word and stand on it, no matter what my body was telling me and how long it took, or I was going to believe none of it. It was time to draw a line in the sand. There was no turning back, wavering, or double-mindedness. It was all or nothing.

I remember the actual moment when I made the conscious decision to believe His Word and to stand on it like I never had before. In order to do that, I needed to move past the unbelief and activate (which is much different than obtaining) the unyielding faith of Abraham. Not only did he believe the promise of God, but he was certain of it, regardless of how much his body told him the opposite. You can believe a promise someone gives you with all your heart and yet still not have confidence in the fulfillment of that promise. You'll find yourself saying things like, "I'll believe it when I see it." When it comes to a promise of healing from Father, you may hear yourself say something like, "When I see healing manifest in my body, then I'll know that I'm healed." That is not the faith that allows you to receive and not the faith Abraham demonstrated for us. It was easy for me to see that I needed to grow in confidence so I wouldn't <u>waver.</u> What wasn't so easy was knowing how to do it. I <u>needed Father to show me how.</u>

God pointed out to me in this passage of Scripture that Abraham walked in the confidence I needed. So how did he get that confidence? I was determined to find out.

Romans 4:19 (KJV) tells us Abraham was "<u>not weak in faith</u>" and "he <u>considered not his own body</u> now dead," <u>nor Sarah's inability to have child</u>ren. Since it says he wasn't weak in faith, it makes sense that he was strong in faith. It also says he was one hundred years old, which was twenty-five years after he received the initial promise.

He was strong in faith after twenty-five years of *not* seeing the promise of God manifest itself in his and Sarah's lives. I certainly couldn't say the same about my walk of faith when it came to receiving the promise of healing.

Mindset 2: The key to Abraham's faith—and I believe one of the biggest reasons why many believers don't receive healing—all hangs on that one phrase: "considered not." (There's that word consider again!) His strong faith was determined by what he focused on and, equally, by what he didn't focus on. He took no thought of any fact that presented itself in opposition to the Word he had received from God. God said it, and that settled it for him. He would have a child, and it didn't matter how long it took.

Romans 4:20 (KJV) says Abraham "staggered not at the

promise of God through unbelief." The longer I was sick without seeing the Word working, the more I allowed un-🡒 belief in. I couldn't understand how Abraham didn't stagger after so much time and through so many physical obstacles, but the same way he was strong in faith was the same way he shut the unbelief out. He kept his mind stayed on the promise of God and refused to focus on his or Sarah's physical bodies. He didn't look at his or Sarah's ages, or the fact that neither his nor Sarah's bodies were physically capable of producing children. If there was naysaying chatter telling him he was nuts to believe such an outlandish promise, He didn't listen to it. He was focused on the promise.

For Abraham, truth trumped fact.

A. W. Tozer gives a great description of unbelief: "Unbelief is actually perverted faith, for it puts its trust not in the living God but in dying men."[1] In a nutshell, Abraham put his faith in God, not in his aging body.

Not only did he not stagger, but verse 20 says he gave glory to God through the whole journey. In my heart of hearts was the belief that Father promised healing to me, but not following Abraham's example led to my not seeing the same results. There was doubt in my heart because my body wasn't reflecting the promise, and there wasn't any praise taking place because I wasn't seeing a single thing change or improve. The praise comes after the healing, right? Determined to be like Abraham, I praised God and thanked Him for my healing, despite the fact that nothing had changed in my body. Results or no results, I was determined to praise Him. After all, nothing says you're healed like praising God before you see it!

F. F . Bosworth said it best when he described the imprisonment of Paul and Silas: "Paul and Silas sang praises at midnight with their backs bleeding and their feet in the stocks, and God sang bass with an earthquake, which set them free."[2] Find a way to praise Father in the middle of your situation, and watch that situation shake and experience those chains coming off.

Abraham could praise God because he had the God-kind of faith (and that was under the old covenant!). He had faith to call those things that were not as though they were. He couldn't see it in the natural, but he could see it in the supernatural. I believe that if he had focused on his physical body, or Sarah's for that matter, then unbelief could have slipped in and prohibited him from receiving God's promise. If unbelief could stop Abraham from receiving, it could certainly stop me from receiving.

Bingo! I took a hard look at what I was "considering" and realized I was spending a lot of time catering to my body and how it felt. The first thing I'd do before I got out of bed in the morning was a quick head-to-toe assessment of how I was feeling and what was hurting. I'd look at my hands and fingers to assess the level of swelling for the day. I'd move around a bit to see how my lower back was feeling. I was spending more time in God's Word and getting more *But*- and more revelation as time passed, but every time I gave attention to something going on in my body, that meant I was giving less attention to what God's Word said about that particular situation. Every time I focused on the pain, I was creating unbelief.

Although faith and unbelief can coexist, my unbelief

was counterbalancing my faith and making it ineffective. I look at faith and unbelief like the scales of justice, with faith on one side and unbelief on the other. Focusing on God's Word creates more weight on the faith side. Focusing on your body and circumstances creates more weight on the unbelief side. The unbelief side is where I was adding more, or at least an equal amount of, weight. It doesn't matter how much faith you have if you have the same amount of unbelief on the other side. They will counteract each other, and you won't see any results one way or the other. You can have gargantuan faith, but that is easily countered by gargantuan unbelief. By the same token, if you have a tiny mustard seed of faith on the scale and zero unbelief, that faith is going to tip the scales, and you will see what you're believing for come to pass.

Whether I recognized it or not—and at the time I didn't—focusing on my physical body was creating unbelief, and that unbelief was causing me to stagger. I was wavering. I believed God, but I believed my body more. My scale was tipping in the wrong direction, and I was actually getting worse. Remember what James 1:6–8 says, that a person who wavers should not expect to receive anything from God because he is "double-minded and unstable." That's what I was: double-minded. There were many promises from God's Word that said He had already healed me. That's all I should have been focused on.

Romans 4:21 is a very powerful Scripture for me. It says Abraham was fully persuaded. The word *fully* in the *Strong's Concordance* means "to carry through to the end."[3] He had absolutely not one single doubt in his mind or heart that what God had promised him He could carry through to the end. He meditated on the promise he had, and he didn't look to his flesh. He denied any thought or circumstance that came against what he knew to be true, and that truth was that God had promised him a child.

He didn't look to the what-ifs or the whens,
but he looked to the absolute—God's promise.

Like Abraham, I needed a promise of my own to anchor my hope on, so I asked myself, what has Father promised me? I didn't have a specific Scripture I felt was mine, so I started reading every healing Scripture I could find. I soon realized, however, that there were so many Scriptures on healing (I had compiled a list of 101), it became overwhelming to get through them every day. I found myself reading through that list just to read it. I didn't know which Scripture would be "the one" to heal me, and I was afraid if I didn't read them all, I would miss it. Occasionally, I'd hear Father try to say something to me, but I'd say, "Wait until I'm finished! I have thirty-six more to read!"

Don't get me wrong, quoting Scripture is profitable when done with the right motivation. Fear of missing something is not the right motivation in any circumstance. Fear had me so wrapped up in doing, I'd forgotten about being. Being in relationship with Father has nothing to do with vain repetition and spiritual checklists. Because I was so doggedly focused on knowing God's promise for me concerning healing, my fear of missing it escorted my search for that promise right into the trap of legalism, performance-based earning of God's grace and thinking something I could do would make my healing manifest. In my mind, if I didn't find His specific Word for me, I wouldn't see my healing. That very thinking kept me from hearing His Word for me and, I believed, gave me the right to tell Him to wait until I was finished with my list.

That's messed up.

He was trying to tell me exactly what it was I was asking for, and I was so focused on what I was doing that I pushed Him to the back burner.

Eventually, I recognized this fear in me and what it was causing me to do, so when I felt that next nudge from Father to stop on a certain Scripture, I did. In the past when I would come across a Scripture that jumped out at me, I would just keep reading because I really didn't know what else to do with it. Now I take those four principles I shared with you and apply them to that Scripture. Without fail, I will get whatever it is Father is trying to communicate to me. *Remove Distractions - Ask 4 wisdom - Pray in the Spirit His Word in the Forefront of UR MIND*

So, as I looked through those 101 healing Scriptures, I asked Father to open my eyes to the Scripture that held my healing. When the first Scripture jumped off the page at me, I shifted my thinking and considered it a word for me from Father—a promise. I prayed about it, meditated on it (filled my mind with the Scripture), and studied it by doing a word study. A typical word study for me looked like this: I would go to blueletterbible.org and look up the verse I was focused on.[4] There is a *Tools* button next to the verse that you can click and it will give you links for the definitions of the words in that verse. I would take words from the definition and put them back into the Scripture, which made it more understandable and relatable to me. It's as simple as that! After the word study, I kept the Scripture running repeatedly in my mind, and I didn't let it go until the importance of that Word was revealed to me as it related to my situation.

Although I had already been searching, working, trying, and doing, it wasn't until this point in my healing journey that the importance of making Scripture my own clicked. For me, it was Romans 8:11 (KJV): "But if the Spirit of him that raised up Jesus from the dead dwell in you, he that raised up Christ from the dead shall also quicken your mortal bodies by his Spirit that dwelleth in you."

That was my Scripture. It was mine. I was taking it and owning it. I was making that Word my flesh.

My thyroid was dead. My immune system was slowly killing me. I knew that I knew that I knew—in "my knower"—that Scripture would be one I could stand on for my healing. I had heard God about the importance of this Scripture. I knew it in my Spirit, and my mind was agreeing. I had quoted this very Scripture over myself dozens of times in the past, but I'd finally wrapped my brain around the truth that there is more to Scripture than memorizing and quoting it. There is the principle of applying it. I removed all distractions, asked Father to lead me down the path of revelation for this verse, prayed in the Spirit with this verse in mind, and kept it constantly in the forefront of my mind (there's those four practical principles again).

As I prayed and meditated, Father led me to do a word study on that Scripture (applied as described above). In my word study, the Scripture came alive in me. I started with the word *dwell*. According to *Thayer's Greek Lexicon*, the word *dwell* means "to be fixed and operative in your soul."[5]

Let's take it one step deeper.

Fixed means "to be fastened securely in position" (fast, firm),[6] and *operative* means "in force or having effect."[7] I thought those definitions through as they related to Romans 8:11. The conclusion: I needed the Spirit of Him Who raised Jesus from the dead to be securely in position and having an effect in my mind, my will, and my emotions in order for my body to be quickened.

Being able to quote a Scripture obviously doesn't make the Spirit fixed and operative, as evidenced by the fact that I certainly wasn't being quickened at the time. The word *quickened* means "by spiritual power to arouse and invigorate, to cause to live, and to make alive"![8] I love the word *quickened*. It makes me shout "Hallelujah!" even now as I write. Once I had the revelation about surrendering the works mentality and applying the Word so it became my flesh, Romans 8:11 was—and forever will be—*my* promise. By the way, it can be yours too. Every Scripture in all sixty-six books in the Bible can be yours. Take them. Apply them. Possess them.

God promised me that if the Spirit was fixed and operating in my soul, He would make my body to live again. This promise connects directly to the renewing of the mind, leading to the transformation of the body (Romans 12:2). Because of this promise, I had hope, and my activation of *the* measure of faith I was given the second I was born again wasn't far behind.

To get that promise fixed and operating in my soul, I continually prayed it over myself and meditated on it. Day and night that Scripture was running through my head until it became more real to me than the symptoms that were plaguing my body.

If you're like me and need to hear things more than once before you really get it, I'm repeating that one.

Day and night that Scripture was running through my head until it became more real to me than the symptoms that were plaguing my body.

I purposely starved my body of my attention and focused solely on His promise to me. When pain came, I would find myself saying, "Yes, I feel you, but the Word says that by Spiritual power my body is being aroused and invigorated right now in this very hour, in this very second, in this very nanosecond!" Countering physical symptoms with the Word (not with willpower—which eventually exhausts itself) caused me to develop the same confidence Abraham had in God's promise to him, and that confidence caused faith to *activate* inside me.

For so long I had tried to *get* faith, and now it was coming effortlessly through focusing on His promise and eliminating unbelief. Unbelief was slowly eliminated by not looking to my body for confirmation of the truthfulness of the promise and by speaking the Word when I experienced anything contrary to the promise. I developed a bold attitude because I knew God's Word was the absolute truth. I spoke them out loud with a renewed enthusiasm. Romans

unbelief -

8:11 was *mine*, and it would heal me. That Word would become my flesh. I just knew it.

For too long, I had allowed physical symptoms to create unbelief that had caused me to waver. Incorporating God's promise to me into Romans 4:18–21, this became my declaration:

> Father, even when there is no reason for good expectations in the natural, I will keep believing because you have told me that the same Spirit that raised Christ from the dead is bringing my physical body back to life. I am strong in faith, and I will not consider the symptoms in my body, nor the doctor's words, nor the lab reports. I will not stagger over Your promise of healing through any unbelief, but I will stay strong and praise Your Holy Name even before I see it manifest in my body. I am fully persuaded that what You have promised You have performed through the death of Your Son and that it is being brought to completion right now in my body!

When my body was telling me something different than what the Word told me, I didn't care because I knew the Word was true.

That was revelation.

My body had not changed yet, but my mind had. That was the first real victory on my healing journey.

2 Corinthians 5:16 (KJV)

"Wherefore henceforth know we no man after the flesh: yea, though we have known Christ after the flesh, yet now henceforth know we him no more."

(NIV)

"So from now on we regard no one from a worldly point of view. Though we once regarded Christ in this way, we do so no longer."

CHAPTER TEN

Spirit vs. Flesh

Do you remember that major change I experienced in October 2013? After several months of Bible school absorbing the Word, a solid foundation upon truth was being established in my heart. God's voice was more clear to me than ever before, and the revelation of Romans 8:11 had me walking on cloud nine. Despite that progress, in October my body was attacked with the worst respiratory sickness I'd ever experienced.

I should be getting better, not worse!

Sleep eluded me. It was impossible to take a deep breath without fits of coughing and pain. My voice was gone. My job as a court reporter was put on hold because my ears were plugged and my incessant barky-type cough would have been too much of a distraction for my clients. Court reporting requires you to be a fly on the wall, but I was an elephant in the room. This dragged on for weeks with no improvement.

In the face of sickness, however, I noticed a big difference in how I was responding to it. Instead of accepting it and suffering through it as I would have in the past, I got angry.

Actually, I was fighting mad.

I was angry because I knew inside that sickness was directly contrary to the promise of health I had from Father. I was angry because I knew the problem wasn't on His end, but on mine, and I got even more determined than ever to get all the revelation I needed to receive my healing.

Bingo!

I need to point out that the understanding that the problem was on my end did not cause condemnation in me. It was a conviction. There is a great difference between the two. Many people who operate under a performance mentality slip into condemnation that is disguised as taking responsibility. That's the "it's all my fault" mentality. This leads you to take the blame, as well as all the terrible emotions that come with it. Conviction, on the other hand, means you are firmly convinced of what you believe. I was firmly convinced that my not receiving my healing was not on God's end, so that left only me as the reason why I hadn't experienced what Jesus died for me to have. This conviction did not cause me to blame myself. It only led me to search more passionately for the truth.

In the midst of that sickness, I purposed in my heart that the devil would be very sorry for attacking me in this way. I obviously had more to learn about His Word and who I am in Christ or he wouldn't have been able to invade my body like he had. That ignorance had allowed him an inroad into and a foothold onto my body. I was determined to make him pay for it.

To this day, he has yet to figure out that everything he throws at me to slow me down and shake my faith only fuels the fire to draw closer to God and continue the fight.

It only makes me stronger. That's the thing about the enemy. He doesn't know how spiritually stunted he is. Once his name was changed from Lucifer to Satan, and he lost his audience with God, he lost his ability to understand the things of God. He permanently fails the spirit realm equivalency test. This deficiency is exactly what believers should be using against him. Since the enemy can only relate to the soulish and fleshly realms, he remains utterly defeated when we fight him from the victory we already have in the spirit realm.

So, back to October 2013. That anger enabled me to put my head down and charge forward. I was determined to get it for myself, but I also began to think that there could be no greater misery for the devil than for me to get a revelation of healing and then to share it with the world so they could get it too.

Mission possible.

I was home sick for what seemed like the millionth day in a row because I hadn't gotten any sleep due to the congestion and coughing during the night. I was listening to a recorded teaching of a class I had missed by Charis Bible College's founder, Andrew Wommack. I didn't know it at the time, but I was about to hear the phrase that would be the beginning of the permanent end of sickness and disease in my body.

Andrew said, "The reason we don't get healed" (you know he had my attention after that opening) "is because our physical body is more real to us than our spirit man. And if we can just get to where we believe more what is true in the spiritual more than what is true in the natural—not

yup

denying the physical, but believing that the spirit is stronger than the physical, the spirit is the parent realm, the superior realm—if we'll believe that, what's true in the spiritual will become true in the physical."

I wanted to pull Andrew out of that CD player, shake him by the shoulders and yell, "What in the world does that mean? How do I do that?" I had lived in my body for thirty-nine years at that point, and the physical realm was my primary point of reference (as it is for most people). I know Galatians 5:17 says the flesh lusts (wars) against the Spirit, and the Spirit wars against the flesh. Not only were my spirit and flesh not at war with each other but, from what I could tell, they were on a white sandy beach sharing a fruity drink with an umbrella in it! I wanted to throw my hands up in disgust and lay on the couch wallowing in my sickness like usual. Most of the time it's just easier *TRUE That* to give up than to fight, isn't it? But I had a prompting in my spirit telling me that what Andrew had said was important—very important—and I needed to diligently seek what it was God wanted me to find.

I listened to that phrase repeatedly until I heard Andrew speaking it in my head without playing the recording. I wrote the phrase out and put it in the front of my school folder where I would see it all day, every day, as a reminder. I prayed in the Spirit, keeping the spirit versus flesh reality in mind. I asked Father to show me what it meant for my spirit man to be more real to me than my flesh. If I couldn't tell the difference between the two, how was I supposed to see my spirit as more real than my flesh?

I had learned in school that every person is created as

a three-part being: They are a spirit, they have a soul, and they live in a body. I understood the concept and believed it. First Thessalonians 5:23 (NKJV) clearly states that fact:

> Now may the God of peace Himself sanctify you completely; and may your whole spirit, soul, and body be preserved blameless at the coming of our Lord Jesus Christ.

The fact that we live in a body is obvious. The body is easy for us to identify with because we can see and feel it. It's also easy to understand that we have an inner part, which the Bible refers to as a soul. Our soul is our per- *soul* sonality, what makes us who we are as an individual. It is the embodiment of our emotions, our will, our conscience, and our intellect. We can feel emotions. We can feel the strength of our will. Our emotions, like our bodies, are very real to us.

The spirit of a man, on the other hand, can't be per- *spirit* ceived through any of our physical senses, which makes it difficult to identify. It is the intangible part of us. It can't be seen or felt. It's like the wind in that you can see the effects of it, but you can't see the wind itself.

I understood the concept of the three parts, but I still couldn't see them as separate because they are all housed in the one part of my being that I identified with the most: my body. I *needed* a revelation of spirit versus flesh. *Bingo*

But how?

A day later, we had a guest speaker come to school who briefly mentioned 2 Corinthians 5:16 in his teaching. It was such a minor point in his teaching, but it jumped out at me like a jack-in-the-box, and I didn't hear a single word of what he said for the rest of the hour after that.

> Wherefore henceforth know we no man after the flesh: yea, though we have known Christ after the flesh, yet now henceforth know we him no more. (2 Corinthians 5:16 KJV)

The New International Version says it like this: "So from now on we regard no one from a worldly point of view. Though we once regarded Christ in this way, we do so no longer."

When I heard that verse, it stopped me dead in my tracks and a thought process began: The disciples knew Jesus in the flesh, but I have never known Him in the flesh. I have never seen His physical body with my eyes, nor heard His voice with my ears, nor touched His actual scars with my hands. Yet, I know Him. I know Him more intimately than I know anyone else in the world. In fact, I probably know Him better than I know myself.

How do I know Him? Through the Word, which reveals His nature, His character, and His will for me. Through the Word, how He'll respond in any situation can be known. I know Him not by His *flesh*, but by His *Spirit*!

Light bulb moment coming . . .

So, Father was telling me that if I can know Jesus in Spirit through the Word, then through the Word is how I would get to know *my* spirit, and how *my* spirit would become real to me. Second Corinthians 5:16 says to know no man after the flesh. Well, I am "no man." "No man" includes me. I am not to know *myself* after the flesh. And just as I know Jesus, I can know the true me, my spirit, through the Word.

I was starting to get it. God is so faithful when we seek Him and ask Him for understanding.

During that same class, as I was thinking about 2 Corinthians 5:16, Father gave me an image that made the separation between my spirit and my flesh very real to me.

I saw an image of a vase with a beautiful flower growing *illustration* out of it. I heard Father say that the vase is just an object, and that it has no life of its own. It is simply the vessel that holds the life, which is the flower. Without the flower, the vase has no purpose and no significance. He was showing me that the vase is my body and the flower is my spirit. My physical body is simply the vessel that holds my spirit. Without my spirit, my body ceases to live. Without my spirit, my body can be dressed up, fattened up, thinned down, broken, or whatever, but it still has no life. The only purpose of the vase is to contain the flower growing inside.

I dug into the Word to find out what it said about my spirit. My search started with John 3:3–8. This is the story of Jesus explaining to Nicodemus that he had to be born again to see and enter into the kingdom of God. Jesus explained there was a difference between being born physically and being born again spiritually.

Have you ever stopped and thought about how crazy Jesus must have sounded to people back in the day? I mean, we have teachers to explain things to us, but the stuff coming from Jesus was fresh off the press! It makes me laugh every time I think about it. Anyway, His point was that when I accepted Jesus as my Lord and Savior, it was my spirit that was born again.

These verses showed me what the Word says about my born-again spirit:

Galatians 4:6 (NKJV) says, "And because you are sons, God has sent forth the Spirit of His Son into your hearts, crying out, 'Abba, Father!'" This Scripture told me when I was born again, God put Jesus' Spirit into my heart. His Spirit is actually in my heart!

Even better, 1 Corinthians 6:17 (NKJV) says, "But he who is joined to the Lord is one Spirit with Him." Not only is His Spirit in my heart, but our spirits are joined together as one. Wow. If my spirit is one with Jesus, then my spirit is perfect and complete—as is His.

First John 4:17 (NKJV) says, "Because as He is, so are we in this world." As Jesus is, so am I in this world. I am positive that Jesus' Spirit does not doubt, and that Jesus' measure of faith is perfectly activated. His Spirit is as perfect as His flesh was sinless, and as He is, so am I right now in this world.

#Bam.

The last of the Scriptures I studied was John 6:63 (KJV), which says, "It is the spirit who quickeneth; the flesh profiteth nothing." It is my spirit that gives this body life. If my spirit left my body to go be in the presence of Jesus, my body would fall down dead. According to James 2:26, without my spirit, my body is nothing. Wow. Meditate on that one for a while and see if your thinking doesn't drastically change.

I don't remember how long I meditated on those

Scriptures, but I know the exact moment when spirit versus flesh became revelation to me. It involved an experience I haven't shared with many people (until now), as many may think I've lost my marbles. But this experience made everything I had been studying and meditating on a reality in my life, so it can't be left untold.

wow – I was standing at my sink one night washing dishes, the water running over my hands, when I looked down and realized I couldn't feel the water anymore. I could see I was still washing the dish I was holding, but I couldn't feel the dish in my hands. The best way to describe it is as an out-of-body experience, but my spirit never left my body. It was like seeing myself from the inside out. In that moment, Father told me He was allowing me to experience the separation between my spirit and my flesh. For a brief instant, I was totally in my spirit and my flesh became nothing. Then, a moment later, I was washing dishes again. Just like that.

I had never experienced anything like that before, and I haven't since. But the truth was revealed. I am a spirit, and my spirit is the true me. When you look at me, you see my body, my shell. But to see the true essence of my being, you have to look at me with your other pair of eyes—the eyes of your spirit.

James 4:7 (NKJV)

"Therefore submit to God.
Resist the devil and he will flee from you."

CHAPTER ELEVEN

The "Domino Effect"

Domino Effect:

> A situation in which one event causes a series
> of similar events to happen one after another.

The revelations I had been receiving—especially the revelation that my spirit was the true me—was creating a "domino effect" that was causing major breakthroughs in my healing journey. Large boulders that had blocked my path to receiving were beginning to crumble, and cracks of light were shining through.

You may be saying, *That's great that you got that revelation about your spirit, but what did you do with it once you had it? What did that look like in your everyday life? How did it lead to you receiving your healing?*

I had the revelation, but now it was time to put it into practice in how I lived, how I spoke, and how I thought so it could become an active part of my life—spirit, soul, and body.

In the day-to-day of how I lived, I consciously tried to respond from my spirit as opposed to reacting in my flesh. *your spiritual identity* That was, and still is, challenging, and I wasn't always successful. My flesh wanted to react and get offended or lash out at the most trivial things. My spirit, on the other hand, wanted to respond in love and patience. In every circumstance, I had a choice: respond or react. When a situation presented itself, I would stop and think before reacting as I normally would (which was usually in the flesh). In the beginning, I had to force myself to respond in the spirit. It was not natural for me. The remnants of that old sin nature wanted to hang on like white on rice. But every time I made the right choice, it became easier and easier to live out of my spirit man.

It's like exercising. When you first get started, it is ridiculously hard—and painful—to do it, but after a while it becomes a healthy habit. Likewise, responding in the spirit was hard—and painful—to do, but the more I practiced it, the more dominant my spirit man got.

Effortless Change

As I exercised my spirit over my flesh, I noticed the words I spoke were effortlessly changing. I used to say things like, "Well, I know I'm healed, but I still have this pain." Or "I know I'm healed, but I haven't seen the manifestation of it yet." I might as well have been saying, "I know I'm healed, but I really must not be yet because I haven't seen it in my body. I'm still waiting for the healing to come." When I talked like that, I was saying I didn't

The real truth comes out —

really believe what I was confessing. Those statements said I didn't really believe I was already healed by the finished work of the cross.

From that revelation, though, came the knowing that my spirit man is the true me, and it is already completely healed.

Amen to that —

I *am* healed already, no matter what my body says, and I'm not waiting on a thing.

Don't get me wrong, it's okay to recognize that

something isn't right in your body. It's not about denying the symptoms. However, your language about that problem needs to change. I noticed I was beginning to say things like this instead: "Okay. I feel you, pain, but *my God says* in Isaiah 53:4 that He carried pain for me so I didn't have to!" And "I see you, swelling, but *my God says* the same Spirit that raised Christ from the dead is fixed and operating in my mind, my will, and my emotions, and He is right now bringing my physical body to life by His supernatural power!" As I put this language into practice, I was getting a revelation of the power of my words, and I could feel my spirit growing stronger as I spoke His Word out loud over my body. I knew what His promises meant, and I was telling my body all about it.

where's your BUT

My thought life was the biggest part of me that was affected by the revelation of spirit versus flesh. How did it change my thought life and lead to my healing? I began to look at the diseases that were in my body very differently. From my study, I knew that lupus, Sjögren's syndrome, hypothyroidism, and all the other diagnoses spoken over me were living inside of my flesh, not in my spirit, because my spirit is perfect. And <u>since my spirit is the real me, where my life comes from—and it cannot hold sickness—then those diseases were not part of the real me.</u> I started thinking of the diseases as <u>not belonging to</u> me. They were no longer my Sjögren's syndrome, my lupus, and my thyroid problem. It wasn't my medication. I thought of and referred to them as what they <u>truly were: enemies, intruders, thieves, and trespassers on the temple of the Holy Ghost</u> (1 Corinthians 6:19). As a result of this changed thinking, I actively resisted them.

Aha Moment

Look at it like this: Imagine you're sitting on your couch with a bowl of popcorn watching a movie. Sitting next to you is the one you love most. It could be your child, your spouse, or your pet. Now imagine someone banging on your front door. They are trying to break in, and you know their intention is to hurt or kill the loved one by your side. I guarantee you would meet that intruder at the front door, weapon in hand, and you would fight with everything you had to protect your loved one. You would fight to save them until you drew your last breath, or until you had defeated the enemy completely, leaving him either dead or running down the street screaming.

You need the same resolve when it comes to attacks on your physical body. Your body is your home. It is where the Holy Ghost resides. Sickness is the enemy trying to break in and steal what is rightfully yours through the new covenant: divine health (which includes the whole kit and caboodle of forgiven sins, healing, prosperity, redemption, and peace).

It's time to get off that couch, break out of your passivity, and stand up against what is trying to destroy you. With the mightiest weapon of them all in hand, the Word of God, fight! Stir yourself up against this enemy and take back what he has stolen. Use the Word to cut the enemy down and put him back in his place.

I know for me that, after so many years of being sick, I had identified with that sickness. It had easily broken in the front door and was now eating my popcorn and deciding what movie to watch. I had accepted it as a part of me. It defined me. It determined what I was or wasn't going to do that day. It was actually determining the course of my life and telling me who I could and couldn't be. It was the ultimate reason I quit being a nurse, a job I loved. Nevertheless, I finally got it through my head and started declaring out loud that sickness is not a part of me. It is not who I am. It does not define me. It's not who you are either.

To focus on the real me, I looked deep into my eyes in the mirror. I know it sounds weird, but just go with it. When I looked into my eyes, I saw past the exterior I could see and feel that held pain and disease, and I was catching a glimpse of the light in my spirit.

I'm challenging you to make a stand now and disown whatever diagnosis you've given permission to stay. Say enough is enough. Disconnect yourself from the symptoms. Don't claim this junk any longer. It is not yours. Declare that out loud, and let your body hear it. Say it one million times a day if you have to. Just do it.

I eventually got to the point where I was ready to tell the sickness and disease in my body who was boss—and really mean it. I had been run over by that junk for way too many years, and had been putting up with way too much of the enemy's nonsense. Struggle is optional. So is sickness.

With a renewed vengeance, I began attacking the symptoms in my body with the Word. I came across a prayer Bob Yandian posted on Facebook, and it became a part of my daily prayer life:

> I am the righteousness of God in Christ Jesus.
> My righteousness came by faith in the finished
> work of Jesus, not by my own works. My righ-
> teousness speaks and declares that I am holy

ground; the temple of the Holy Spirit. My righteousness is eternal. I am not a sinner getting rid of sin. I am the righteous resisting temptations. I am healed. I was healed at the Cross by the stripes of Jesus. Jesus has already taken my infirmities and borne my sicknesses. If Jesus took and bore them, I need not bear them. I have been healed since I was saved. My healing is eternal. Nothing can change that. I am not the sick trying to be healed. I am the healed resisting symptoms of infirmity and disease. I have been bought with a price, I will therefore glorify God in my body. Sickness is an unholy enemy trying to stand on holy ground, a trespasser on private sacred property and a thief in the temple of the Holy Spirit.

In Jesus' name, I forbid my body to be deceived in any manner. Body, you will not be deceived by any germ, disease, or virus. Neither will you work against life or health in any way. Every cell of my body supports life and health!

God has sent His Word and healed me and delivered me from all of my afflictions. His promises are medicine and healing to all my flesh. The anointing of the Holy Spirit has also been sent to heal every part of my being, emotional and physical. The same Holy Spirit who raised Jesus from the dead quickens my mortal body. No plague will come near my dwelling because I abide under the shadow of the almighty. Jehovah Rapha is my covenant healer, and with the stripes of Jesus I was and

am healed. SICKNESS, LEAVE MY BODY
IN JESUS' NAME.

I started speaking this and declaring it over my body
every day. I could feel my spirit getting stronger, and the
effects of the symptoms losing power with every word. The
tides were turning as my spirit took over and death was
losing its grip on me.

However, despite the revelations I had received and
the changes I was making in my behavior, words, and
thoughts, there was still no change in my body. After living
my whole life depending on my senses to tell me if I was
healthy or not, it was taking some time for my mind to become renewed to the fact that it was now my spirit who was
running the show. It seemed like every time I "got" something, I would get sicker. I know many of you can relate.

I realize now that the devil was desperate to keep me
from receiving my healing, and he was throwing everything
he could at me because I was getting closer. So if you take
one step forward and then seem to get thrown two steps
backward, take heart and be encouraged that you're on the
right path. Keep after it. Don't give up. Don't lose heart.
Laugh at the devil; tell him you've got his number and that
you won't be stopped. Submit to God's Word that you're
healed, resist the devil, and he *will* flee from you (James
4:7).

You'll win if you don't quit.

2 Corinthians 5:21 (NKJV)

"For He made Him who knew no sin to be sin for us, that we might become the righteousness of God in Him."

CHAPTER TWELVE

Over the Moon

"Just because you can't see it
doesn't mean it isn't all there."
~God

The respiratory sickness I had been standing and fighting against continued into Christmas of that year and worsened on a trip to Georgia my husband and I took to visit family. We both agreed if I wasn't better by the time we got back from our trip that I would go see the doctor. It was going on two months, and the coughing was uncontrollable. I was barely sleeping. By the way, where does all that snot come from? Seriously, it was ridiculous! My flesh may have still been in control, but I could feel a shift in my spirit. Every day I spent focused on the Word, my spirit had more dominion over my thoughts. The sickness was irritating and it was disrupting my activities, but I was beginning to see past the obvious distraction of it. I was beginning to believe what I couldn't see.

We were driving one night on the four-day journey to Georgia, and God showed me something tangible that solidified what I was already beginning to believe about my healing. (Kind of like how God had Abram look at the stars in Genesis 15:5 to give him a visual of the scope of the promise He made to him.) I was staring out the car window, gazing up at the beautiful crescent moon. As I looked at it, I heard Father say in His simple yet profound way, "Just because you can't see it doesn't mean it isn't all there." It dawned on me that even though I could only see a small portion of the moon with my natural eyes, I knew beyond a shadow of a doubt that it was all there. There was no doubt the moon was full even though I couldn't see it, and there was nothing you could say to me that would convince me otherwise. It is a truth.

The fact is: I couldn't see the full moon with my natural eyes. The truth is: The full moon was there. At that time, in my body, I was seeing no moon at all in reference to my healing. Not even a sliver. Actually, my healing looked like the equivalent of a pitch black, moonless night. I knew in my heart, though, that He was trying to help me understand that my healing was most definitely there regardless of what I was seeing—or not seeing—in my body.

Through that simple illustration, I became confident that even though I didn't have the manifestation of my healing, I knew it was there as sure as I knew the moon was in the sky. And just like Abram, every time I saw the moon, I was reminded of His promise that I was healed. My healing was there—completely.

I had heard from my Father, and the faith that came from hearing began to squash the unbelief my body had been causing. Faith is knowing you're healed even when your body tells you you're not. Faith is putting more weight on what God's Word says about your healing than what your body is screaming at you. Faith is believing it before you see it. Faith is knowing the moon is there even when it has no illumination from the sun.

We finally arrived in Georgia after four days of driving, and by that time I was miserable physically. But spiritually, I was awake inside and growing stronger every day, despite the pain in my body from the travel and the incessant coughing and congestion. I decided to take a walk one day and headed out alone down an isolated dirt road. I was walking slowly and extremely limited by what my lungs would allow me to do. My body didn't feel like it (the importance of ignoring feelings is another entire book by itself), but I started speaking healing Scriptures out loud. I'd had a revelation about these Scriptures (the same ones I mentioned in chapter 6), but something different was happening as I spoke them out this time.

As I spoke the Word, I felt my spirit begin to stir within me. There was a noticeable change in my tone, and I began to repeat those same Scriptures with authority in my voice. One of the instructors at Charis says, "When you know, you speak, and you speak with authority because authority flows from revelation." I was experiencing the authority that flows from revelation for the first time in my life.

Speaking those healing Scriptures transformed into declarations of who I was and what belonged to me. "I am a child of God. I am the righteousness of God in Christ." Then with boldness, "I am an heir, and therefore all God's promises belong to me, and nothing can keep them from me!" I was shouting at the top of my lungs—cracking voice, cough, and all—crying that ugly cry while laughing and thanking God for the revelation that had just been birthed in me. I was being those Scriptures. What I was saying about righteousness and being a child of God were as much a part of me as the color of my eyes.

So were the promises of healing. I'd had head knowledge of it before, but it was becoming a revelation to my soul (mind, will, emotions) with every step I took and every word that came out of my mouth.

I *am* a child of God.

Those promises were mine because of who I am. Being a co-heir with Jesus had nothing to do with anything I had done, but I was righteous simply because when Father looks at me, He only sees the perfection of His Son.

I *am* righteous before God (2 Corinthians 5:21).

Some may think that sounds heretical, but it's the truth, so I'll say it again: I am righteous!

On that walk, who I am in Christ became a reality to me. I confessed what I believed, and took hold of the healing He had set before me. Before that day, I'd had revelation that all those promises were mine, that they were there for me all along, but I hadn't yet taken them for myself.

A word on "taking it": Imagine you are hot and thirsty. There is a nice glass of cold water sitting in front of you. You know that it is water. You know when you drink it you won't be thirsty any longer. So you sit there and you look at the glass. You keep looking at it. You tell the glass of water you're thirsty. You keep looking at it. You ask the glass why you're still thirsty. You keep looking at it. You wait for the glass to do something. You keep looking at it.

TAKING it

Until you reach out, take hold of it for yourself and drink from that glass, your thirst will never be quenched.

Father has set before you healing, but you must reach out and take it. You can't sit passively back and wait for it. You have to actively pursue what God has promised you.

How?

Do you remember chapter 3? If not, go back and read it again. Remove distractions, ask for revelation, pray in the Spirit, and keep the Word in the forefront of your mind.

When I got a revelation that day of who I was in Christ (I am a daughter of the Most High God and a joint heir with Jesus, woo-hoo!), my mind was renewed and I was able to take hold of Father's promise of healing.

After that walk out in the middle of nowhere, I knew that I knew that I knew (yep, in "my knower") that healing was mine. I walked back to the house victorious with my chin up. I knew a spiritual battle had been won. If I could have seen into the spirit realm, I have no doubt that the angels who have charge over me were celebrating a great victory and rejoicing with me.

After having the respiratory sickness for several months, my cough almost immediately began to disappear. Within a few days, it was completely gone. I was seeing the Word-seeds I had planted becoming active in my soul, and the harvest was happening in my body.

Did it surprise me that I prayed and saw healing come to my body within a short amount of time? No, because that's exactly what is supposed to happen. In the past, however, I have to admit that it would have surprised me to see such quick results. Ask yourself this: If you were to pray for someone who was paralyzed in a wheelchair, and they were to get up and walk as soon as you finished praying, would you be shocked? Come on, be honest. I can tell you that absolutely would have been my old reaction. Why do we respond that way?

I didn't understand it at the time, and wouldn't realize it until sometime later, but I would have reacted that way because my heart was hardened when it came to healing. I believe this hardening was caused by the length of time I had been believing, speaking, standing, quoting, praying, and studying and not seeing any results. Delays in what you are believing for can cause wavering, despair, and discouragement if you are not rooted and grounded in His Word and love. Proverbs 13:12 (NKJV) says, "Hope deferred makes the heart sick." I think heart sickness is not dissimilar from sickness that lingers in the body. I also think heart sickness can be more difficult to cure. After all, out of the heart flows the issues of life (Proverbs 4:23). Issues can work for or against us.

Father revealed the hardness of my heart to me one day when I was watching television. Yes, He can even speak through television. An evangelist was on a program talking about the miraculous things that would happen during his meetings. He testified of people losing weight and becoming a few sizes smaller instantly (um, okay), new teeth appearing, people growing taller, full heads of hair growing instantly, and many other miraculous things.

The skeptic in me responded immediately with, "Yeah, right, like that really happened." Just as quickly as

Me too!

I responded, I heard Father say, "Do you not believe I can do those things?"

Huh? Wow.

I really thought about what He had asked me. Did I not believe that He is the God of the miraculous? Did I not believe that He has the power to do those things? The lame walk, the deaf hear, and the blind see because of Him. I was putting His power in a box that was limited to the size of my peanut brain. While His power is immeasurable, we can limit Him. (Check out Psalm 78:41 on that one.)

Through the television chat God had with me, that peanut brain of mine figured out I shouldn't be amazed when I pray and it works. I shouldn't be amazed when miraculous healings take place. Instead, I should be amazed when my prayer doesn't work, when my body doesn't obey, and I should expect to see miracles take place. Healing should be an everyday occurrence in the life of a believer, and we should get to the point where we're surprised when it doesn't happen. When we speak the name of Jesus, all of hell should tremble and things should happen.

Hardness of heart is illustrated in Mark 6:48–52 (KJV):

> And he saw them toiling in rowing; for the wind was contrary unto them: and about the fourth watch of the night he cometh unto them, walking upon the sea, and would have passed by them.
>
> But when they saw him walking upon the sea, they supposed it had been a spirit, and cried out:

> For they all saw him, and were troubled.
> And immediately he talked with them, and
> saith unto them, Be of good cheer: it is I; be
> not afraid.
> And he went up unto them into the
> ship; and the wind ceased: and they were sore
> amazed in themselves beyond measure, and
> wondered.
> For they considered not the miracle of the
> loaves: for their heart was hardened.

Jesus ordered the disciples to get into their ship and cross over to the other side to Bethsaida. They had a difficult time crossing because of the wind, and Jesus had to rescue them. He was out taking a leisurely stroll on the water when He saw them, and then calmed the wind with His words. They were astonished. They were beside themselves. Their jaws were on the floor of the ship. Why? Because they "considered not" (there's that word again in verse 52) the miracle they had just witnessed (that same day!) of Jesus feeding the crowd of five thousand with five loaves and two fish. They were so focused on the storm they were going through, they placed more value on their physical circumstances than on the miracle they had just seen Him perform.

If you are shocked when miraculous healings happen, you have a hardened heart.

That's a tough one to admit, but it's not all bleak. You can change that hardness of heart by considering—meditating on, focusing on, fixing your eyes on—the things of God as opposed to the things of this world. Spend more time with your attention fixed on God and His promises (which are *all* for your good and His glory) than you do on the things of the world and the symptoms in your body. Your heart will become sensitive in the area of healing.

I practiced "considering" by focusing on the Gospels and reading about all the wonderful miracles and healings that took place during Jesus' short ministry here on the earth. I saw God's power in action through the hands (and heart) of Jesus. I focused on the things He'd already done in my life, and on the things that had changed. I stopped focusing on those things that hadn't changed. I chose to fix my eyes on the improvement I had seen in my body, and not on what was left to be fixed.

Hardness of heart kept me from seeing the Word I believed down to my core from manifesting in my body. Fear and doubt that accompanied the symptoms and the diagnoses (i.e., the lies) that had been spoken over me took center stage—much like the disciples were overcome with the fear that came from being in a ship that was being knocked about by the wind. Instead of being alive to the mighty way God's Word had already been working in my life, my focus was on the circumstances. It wasn't on the victories I had already seen or on the battles that had already been won in my soul and in my body. My thoughts were set more on the things that increase fear and doubt than on the power of His Word.

So I committed to stop thinking about the lupus, thyroid problems, and everything else that was still in my body. Instead, my attention shifted to how the power of the Word had defeated the respiratory sickness that had plagued me for months. For me, the defeat of that illness was like the feeding of the five thousand. It was a miracle, and I stayed in that lane. Beating that illness was a flat-out spirit versus flesh battle. It was a battle of positioning truth over fact in my body. I had experienced exactly what Andrew Wommack said would happen when my journey began: My spirit man had become the dominant realm, and what was true in my spirit had become reality in my flesh. A major victory had been won, and the war was about to be over.

Numbers 13:33 (NKJV)

"There we saw the giants
(the descendants of Anak came from the
giants); and we were like grasshoppers in our
own sight, and so we were in their sight."

CHAPTER THIRTEEN

Friday Night Fights

I left Georgia after our Christmas vacation with an entirely new attitude because of the battle I'd won there. I no longer had the whiny-voiced, when-am-I-going-to-be-healed attitude, and I was developing some spiritual "swag." I had some moxie in my words and in my step. I no longer saw myself as the sick trying to get well, but as the healed resisting the sickness in my body. I felt like superwoman, like I could go out and conquer the world. I had spoken to my body and for the first time in my life, it not only listened, but it responded.

Of course it did. I'm a child of God.

Before that experience, when I spoke the Word over my body, nothing happened because there was no power to back up the words I spoke. They were empty. It was like swinging at a baseball without a bat—all air and no power. My words were hot air.

Don't misunderstand me. The Word itself had all the power it needed for me to be healed, but the words that came from my mouth didn't encompass that power. The Word had authority, but I didn't. Before that day, 2 Corinthians 5:21 was a verse in my repertoire, but there was no power when I spoke it because I didn't have true understanding of its meaning. Luke 10:19 declared that authority had been given to me to tread on serpents and scorpions, and over *all* the power of the enemy, but there was a lack of understanding about what authority meant or how to use it. So, again, they were just words, and when I spoke them the devil didn't tremble and flee because he could see right through me. I didn't know who I was, nor the authority I had, so that equaled no power to speak to disease and see it leave.

The following story will help illustrate how many Christians diminish their authority. Father helped me develop this story based on Mark 4:35–40. It is a passage of Scripture I had heard many times but not from this perspective. He asked me to look beyond what I knew about it on the surface and to think about what that story would look like in my everyday life. It opened up my eyes to the fact that even though I knew who I was, I didn't know my authority. So I'm going to ask you to imagine this scenario in your mind, as I did, and envision yourself as the main character in the story. Consider this question as you read the passage and then the story: how do I see myself?

First, Mark 4:35–40 (NLT):

> As evening came, Jesus said to his disciples, "Let's cross to the other side of the lake."
>
> So they took Jesus in the boat and started out, leaving the crowds behind (although other boats followed).
>
> But soon a fierce storm came up. High waves were breaking into the boat, and it began to fill with water.

Jesus was sleeping at the back of the boat with his head on a cushion. The disciples woke him up, shouting, "Teacher, don't you care that we're going to drown?"

When Jesus woke up, he rebuked the wind and said to the waves, "Silence! Be still!" Suddenly the wind stopped, and there was a great calm.

Then he asked them, "Why are you afraid? Do you still have no faith?"

Now the story. It's a Friday night fight. (My dad and I used to watch boxing together when I was younger, so I could see this immediately in my mind's eye.) It's time for the main event, and you suddenly find yourself standing center stage and in the spotlight. You realize you are the main event and that this is the fight of your life. You look down, see the gloves on your hands and you're wearing those shiny shorts boxers always wear. You look to your corner and see your cornerman. It's Jesus. You look to the opposite corner to see your opponent. You guessed it; it's the devil.

Now, you can see this scenario in one of two ways. Following is how I believe the disciples would have seen it, and unfortunately how many believers today see it. Your cornerman, Jesus, is meek, lowly, and humble. Maybe even effeminate. He's standing with His hands folded in front of Him with His head down. He's wearing a flowing white robe and not making eye contact with anyone except for the occasional glance at you and your opponent. He's the gentle, blonde-headed, blue-eyed picture we've all seen with Him holding a lamb in His arms. He's the powerless man hanging on the cross in physical defeat. He's weak. Get the picture?

In the other corner is the devil. He is at least fifteen feet tall and red all over with bulging muscles that would put Arnold Schwarzenegger, in his prime, to shame. He has horns that are sharp enough to impale you in a second and talons that could rip you to shreds. He has a tail that snakes around and is so sharp that it could take your head off in the blink of an eye. There is smoke coming out of his nostrils, and his glowing yellow eyes are piercing right through you. Oh yeah, he's also a centaur—half man, half horse—and he is scraping his foot on the ground like a bull ready to charge. He's just waiting for the bell to ring so he can take you apart.

I know it sounds silly, but isn't this really what we think of him?

Now, with that picture in mind, let's look at the disciples first before we relate the story to ourselves. Jesus begins by saying to them, "Let's cross to the other side of the lake." He gives them a word and sends them out. They step into the ring by setting sail.

The devil immediately steps up and says, "Oh, no you don't!" and sends the storm (he always—without fail—intends to challenge a word). The waves beat on the ship. The ship starts to fill with water, and the disciples are in fear. They panic as the devil throws punches at them and swings that scary tail.

They finally go running back to Jesus, who is sleeping like a baby through the storm, and they receive this response: "Why are you afraid? Do you still have no faith?"

They were fearful because they didn't realize the word Jesus spoke (to go to the other side) was actually a promise that they would make it to the other side. He wouldn't say "Let's cross to the other side" if He didn't know was would happen. Had they realized that, they could have simply said to that storm, and the devil in the ring, "Silence! Be still!" and it would have obeyed. Round 1—devil.

So let's use that same viewpoint and see how that would look in your life today. Jesus begins by saying to you: "I want you to drop everything and go to Bible college. I will supply all your needs according to the riches of my Father, and because I am faithful and I have called you, I will do it" (Philippians 4:19; 1 Thessalonians 5:24). With that word, you step out into the ring.

The devil steps forward and hisses, "You can't afford school. How will you pay your bills? What about work? I will crush you, and you'll lose your house and your family. You'll never be worth anything!" All the while he is pushing you back toward your corner.

With shoulders sagging and your head down, you say to Jesus, "Well, if it's God's will, He'll pay my bills so I can go to school." Round 1—devil.

Jesus sends you back out to face your opponent with these words: "Because of My stripes, you are healed" (1 Peter 2:24). You step out into the ring.

The devil quickly lunges forward and screams, "Oh, yeah? Well, your throat hurts and your nose is runny and you're coughing like a veteran smoker! Better yet, you have cancer and I'm going to kill you within a few weeks! Where's your God now?"

Again, you cower back to your corner to stand next to

the weak and lowly Jesus saying, "Well, I know I'm healed, but I sure feel terrible, and the doctor's report doesn't look good. I'd better start getting my affairs in order in case God doesn't come through. Jesus, will You comfort me while I wait for the manifestation of my healing? I just don't know if I'm going to be healed in time."

This attitude is, I believe, why so many Christians are living in defeat, sickness, poverty and depression. They don't know who they are, and they don't know their cornerman! Round 2—devil.

Here's how this story really looks. In our corner, Jesus, in all his majesty and glory. The word *glory* in the Greek is *doxa*, and it means "splendor, brightness, magnificence, excellence"![1] He is strong and powerful, and victory oozes from every pore. He knows He has already won this fight for us. We stand next to our King and He hands us our armor: the full armor of God. We put on the belt, the breastplate, and the helmet. Then He hands us the ultimate weapon: the sword of the Spirit—the Word of God. We know we cannot be defeated. We turn to our opponent, ready for any fight that may come our way, knowing that Jesus backs our every step and our every word that agrees with His Word. We look to the other corner and face our defeated foe.

The corner is empty. Crickets.

In reality, the devil isn't even in the ring with us. To find him you have to leave the ring, go up the arena stairs, out into the foyer, out the entrance doors, and across the parking lot. There you see what you think is your opponent standing in the street, a puzzled look on his face.

He's wondering how to get close enough to you to swing a punch. He is not what you expected at all. He is a cowering, sniveling, naked, tiny little creature. He's scrawny. He's weak. His tail is limply tucked between his legs. He is shaking at the sight of you (because Christ is inside you). But, he's angry. He's angry you're wearing the armor and that you have learned who you are: a child of the King. The little punk is angry that you've figured out he is a defeated foe. I'm not making this up, by the way. The enemy (and how we'll react when we see him) is fully described in the Bible by Isaiah, who was inspired by the Holy Spirit when he recorded his revelation. Isaiah 14:16–17 (NLT) says:

> Everyone there will stare at you [Satan] and ask,
> "Can this be the one who shook the earth
>   and made the kingdoms of the world tremble?
> Is this the one who destroyed the world
>   and made it into a wasteland?
> Is this the king who demolished the world's
> greatest cities and had no mercy on his
> prisoners?"

The day will come when we will look on the devil and, squinting our eyes in disbelief, we'll say, "Are you kidding me? Is this a joke? Is this the one who caused me so many problems?" A perfect example of this is demonstrated in The Wizard of Oz. In the scene when the curtain was pulled back revealing the one who had held so much power and control over everyone and everything, Dorothy and friends were terrified and expecting to see something mystical and horrifying. Meanwhile, it was just a wise old man with the cunning ability to deceive. Likewise, we will be amazed at the puny, feeble weakness of the master of deception. He's not called "the father of lies" for nothing.

But, for the sake of this analogy, let's just say the devil is at least in the ring with you. Same scenario: Jesus sends you out with a promise when He says, "Go to Bible college, and I will supply all your needs according to the riches of my Father." You step out to the middle of the ring to face your opponent.

The bell rings and the devil uses the only weapon he has, deception, and says, "You can't afford school. How will you pay your bills? What about work? I will crush you and you'll lose your house and your family. You'll never be worth anything!"

Instead of shrinking back as you did before, you remember Jesus' promise and say, "No! My God shall supply all my needs according to his riches in glory in Christ Jesus! No! My God gives me the power to get wealth!" (Deuteronomy 8:18). "No! I am seeking the Lord, so I will not want for any good thing!" (Psalm 34:10). And the knockout punch? "My God who has called me is faithful, and He will do it!" (1 Thessalonians 5:24).

Next Jesus sends you out with this promise: "Because of My stripes, you are healed" (1 Peter 2:24). The bell rings. You step out.

The devil lunges forward, in all his silliness, and screams, "Oh, yeah? Well, your throat hurts and your nose is runny and you're coughing like a veteran smoker! Better yet, you have cancer and I'm going to kill you within a few weeks! Where's your God now?"

You turn your back on him, look at Jesus, and say:

"Because of His stripes, I am healed." You turn back and advance toward the devil. "His words are life unto me and health to all my flesh!" (Proverbs 4:22) Your words have knocked him to the ground. You put your foot that is shod with the preparation of the gospel of peace on his neck and say, "He has redeemed me from every sickness, every plague, and every disease!" (Deuteronomy 28:61; Galatians 3:13). Then you're jumping up and down on him just to rub his broken nose in it and saying, "The same Spirit that raised Christ from the dead lives in me and is quickening my mortal body!" (Romans 8:11). You will have the devil running and screaming, tail tucked between his legs, wishing he had never even challenged you. Not only that, but he'll think twice about coming back for another round.

You have to know who you are if you want your words to have authority. Numbers 13:33 (NKJV) says, "There we saw the giants (the descendants of Anak came from the giants); and we were like grasshoppers in our own sight, and so we were in their sight."

Your enemy will see you as you see yourself. Are you a giant or are you a grasshopper? You are the victor. Jesus has already won the battle for you. When you have a promise from God, the only time you'll have to fight with the devil is if you take off your armor and invite him in to duke it out. His Word holds every promise you need to stand victorious in the ring in every area of your life (2 Peter 1:3).

Jesus knew Who He was and He knew Whose He was: He's His Father's Son. That's why at the sound of His voice sickness left, blind eyes were opened, deaf ears could hear, and demons fled.

As a daughter of the Most High God, I know I am an

heir with Jesus. I have a blood-bought right to all of the same promises He has. I have a blood-bought right to everything Father has promised me, and Satan does not have the right to take it.

I made the decision I would accept nothing less than what had been promised to me in His Word. He promised health, not sickness. He promised wealth, not poverty. He promised peace, not fear. When I finally got the revelation of who I was and my standing in His kingdom, my words became more than words: they became *the Word,* and my body had no choice but to respond inkind.

Philippians 2:9–11 (NKJV)

"Therefore God also has highly exalted Him
and given Him the name which is above every
name,
that at the name of Jesus every knee should
bow, of those in heaven, and of those on earth,
and of those under the earth,
and that every tongue should confess that
Jesus Christ is Lord, to the glory of God the
Father."

CHAPTER FOURTEEN

Suddenly

The next several months were spent chewing on the revelations I had received. It was as if God had opened the curtains and sunshine was flooding over me. A new day had dawned. My mind was clear for the first time in my life as the water of the Word washed over me. Seeing, knowing, and living the truth was my new reality. Even though symptoms were still present in my body, they just didn't matter anymore. My focus had shifted from being singularly focused on receiving my healing to asking Father how to share my revelations with others. Though healing had yet to manifest in my body, I was certain others could take what I had learned, apply it to their own lives, and receive the healing *they* believed would manifest. There was no doubt in my mind that was the truth. It is the truth.

I continued to meditate on what I had learned. That time was important, because it was during that time that the roots of revelation went deeper. Not much else happened over the next three months. I didn't receive any new revelation, and my body remained unchanged.

There was one more puzzle piece of revelation I'd discover that would complete my journey.

I was so close, but I didn't know it. If I had quit then—based on the way my body felt—I'd still be in the same position today. Stay the course. Just when you're ready to quit, encourage yourself in the truth that God's best for you is right around the corner.

I knew what His promises meant. I knew I was healed. I knew my standing with Christ. I knew that when Father looked at me, all He saw was the finished work of His Son on the cross. Mindsets had been corrected. Strongholds had been broken. Fear was gone. Hope and faith had been restored.

As March 2014 rolled around, Father really had me thinking about the finished work of the cross. I was single-minded and zeroed-in on Jesus and what He had done for me.

One day Father opened my eyes—through a vision—to the torture, crucifixion, death, burial, and resurrection of my Savior. The end result of this vision was the final piece of my healing journey puzzle. I don't know how long the vision lasted, but I could see it clearly in my mind's eye, and its effect is permanent.

The first thing I saw was Jesus as He stood before His accusers. He was silent as they berated Him and dared Him to defend himself. The Word says He was silent, like a sheep before the shearers (Isaiah 53:7). Have you ever watched a sheep being shorn? Watch a YouTube video on it, and think about our Savior in that position.[1] It will change your perspective forever. He stood accused. And then He looked right at me.

In the vision, I saw Jesus as they forced the crown of

thorns on His head. I saw Him grimace. And He looked at me.

I saw Him being whipped, and the flesh being ripped from His body. All the while, His eyes were locked with mine, as I stood helpless before Him.

I watched as He attempted to carry His cross, wood splinters digging into the gashes on His back. And He looked at me.

I watched in horror as He was nailed to the cross. And He looked at me.

I wept when I heard Him cry out after the cross was mercilessly dropped into the hole in the ground. And He looked at me.

He's hanging on the cross—in indescribable agony—and I can do nothing about it. And He looked at me.

As my eyes are fixed on Him, I felt something happening inside of me. I looked down and saw all the sickness and disease leave my body. It came out of me and went into Jesus. I saw it destroying Him. I saw it eating away at His organs. I saw the deformity and the bulged disk in His back.

But I saw more than the sickness that was in my body.

I saw cancer, scoliosis, broken bones, skin rashes, viruses, bacteria and every trauma the body can suffer.

His eyes were still fixed on mine. He was carrying the sins of the world, but also every sickness and disease that has ever or will ever manifest. He was the perfect sacrifice. He fulfilled the law and freed me from the curse of it.

I watched Him take His last breath, and I was transported with Him into the pit of hell. I saw Satan fall to his face in Jesus' presence, in full submission offering the keys of hell, death and the grave to Him, his hand trembling. The same keys—and authority to rule and reign on this earth—Adam and Eve handed over in the garden of Eden were in Jesus' hand. Jesus has all authority.

We are transported to the right hand of the Father where Jesus is to take His appointed seat next to God the Father. Before He sits, He turns His eyes to me. He reaches out and hands *me* the keys. *Me.* The keys are now in *my* hands. He paid the most excruciating price imaginable for those keys, that authority, and He freely gave them to me. His crucifixion, burial, and resurrection gave His name all authority and power, and now He was giving *me* the authority to use His name. I was overwhelmed at this revelation. I walked in the clouds for days, reliving that vision.

Healing School: March 13, 2014. We were in the middle of praise and worship when these words were spoken from the stage:

"So we were singing about His name. How many of you out here have had something diagnosed, where they've given it a name? Raise your hands."

I raised my hand.

"So a doctor or somebody said, 'This is what you've got,' right? Do you realize that there is enough—more than enough power in the name of Jesus that whatever that name is, whatever that symptom, whatever the pain, whenever it tries to rear its head and tell you it's in control, you don't have to come up with some fancy, eloquent confession. You can simply declare the name of Jesus. You can just simply say out of your mouth, 'Jesus.' You can speak directly to that diagnosis, to that name, and just say the name of Jesus to it. That's all that's needed. There is more than enough power in that one name. One name! So no more keeping your mouth shut! No more staying silent, because you can speak the name of Jesus!"

Yes!

She then had us speak the name of Jesus—just His name—with that diagnosis in mind. We were to speak His name to the thing with a name. I spoke His name.

Then, the final death blow to the diseases in my body came through this word given a few moments later:

"There have been names given to you, but whatever that name is, His name is higher." It's all about the name! "And some of you have been intimidated by names, like autism or what the doctors call 'the big c.' You've made those names big. Well, let me tell you, 'the big c' in their terms is tiny and insignificant compared to our 'Big C.' The Big J.C. And when you take the c away from cancer, what have you got? The 'answer.' Listen, put our 'Big C' over whatever problem you've got today. Whatever that name is, put our 'Big C' over it—the name of Jesus Christ—because He paid the price and will set us free. So put that name above any name!"

That was it. That was the final piece of the puzzle. The authority of His name was the key, and I knew without a doubt from the vision that authority had been given to me. The dominoes of revelation that had been lining up for months began to fall, and the last one down caused an explosion to go off inside me. I spoke to the diseases in my body. "Lupus, you get out of my body in Jesus' name.

Sjögren's syndrome, you leave my body. Back, you be healed. Carpal tunnel, you be healed." I wasn't shouting. I was calm. I had authority to use the name of Jesus, and no sickness, no disease, *nothing* could stand up in the presence of that glorious name when it was spoken from my mouth.

Just like that, I knew it was done. I had received my healing. I praised and worshiped Him.

Within a few minutes I heard Him say (as if He were standing in front of me), "You are healed from the top of your head to the tip of your toes, and you will walk in divine health."

He was matter-of-fact about it. I was so fully persuaded, I didn't even need to hear Him to know I was healed, but it sure was cream cheese icing on the carrot cake to hear it.

I was almost surprised when healing came that day because it had been the furthest thing from my mind for a while. It was ironic that in order to receive what my body needed the most, I had to stop thinking about it. Stop pursuing it. It was in the pursuit of an intimate relationship with my Father that the healing came.

Our relationship was no longer about the healing I needed; it was about getting to know Him.

As I drew closer to Him and His light shone on me, the darkness in my body had no choice but to flee. People frequently ask me when the symptoms stopped, but I really don't know. I was so focused on relationship with Him that if the symptoms were there, I don't remember them.

On the way home from Healing School that day, I heard Father speak again. This time He said, "So if you're healed from the top of your head to the tip of your toes, doesn't that mean your thyroid too?" That stopped me in my tracks. I had been completely dependent upon thyroid medication to function in life since 2001. I had a flashback to telling a good friend of mine a few short months earlier that I was waiting for the day when Father would tell me to stop taking my medication. I knew that day would come. It was here. Now.

Wow.

A tiny bit of fear tried to briefly creep in as the gravity of stopping my medication hit home. I knew what would happen if I *wasn't* healed and I stopped taking it: confusion, muscle cramps and thinning hair (all within a short period of time). But just as quickly as that fleeting thought of fear came, I heard Him say, "I am telling you now that you are healed from the top of your head to the tip of your toes. Will you receive it? Will you believe it?"

My God had now said to me *twice* that I was healed from the top of my head to the tips of my toes. Who was I going to believe: almighty God or doubt and unbelief? If He said it, that settled it!

However, despite all I had heard Him say, I needed more in order to step out onto that tightrope and stop taking my pills.

#Don'tJudgeMyFleece

A word about medication: One of the biggest questions I get is, "Should I stop taking my medication?" My response to that question is always, "If you have to ask me, then you're not ready to stop taking it." You need to be positive that is what Father wants you to do. I took the thyroid and pain medication for thirteen years—without guilt or condemnation—knowing they would keep me functioning every day. That's what I had faith for. The pills didn't represent a lack of faith, but rather a temporary fix to what was wrong with my body.

This is how I feel about medication: If the symptoms in your body are interfering with your work for God and the call He has placed on your life, and that problem can be fixed medically, then go to the doctor. If the spiritual warfare is so strong that faith for healing isn't producing results, then take the medication. You can't be an effective witness if you are racked with pain or are unable to concentrate. Doctors and the Word have the same goal: to make you better. I believe Father gave doctors the ability and the gift of being able to treat the human body. Take the medication, take the treatment, and receive it in faith that it is helping and healing your body. In everything you do, ask Father what is best for you. He knows better than anyone what we need, when we need it, and for how long we need it.

Back to my Gideon's fleece test.

I went home immediately and prayed in the Spirit. I told Father I needed confirmation from Him that He was telling me to stop my medicine and that it was going to need to be something pretty close to an audible voice from heaven. I was *not* going to stop unless I was 100 percent certain I was hearing from God. Stopping wasn't going to be a test to see if I was really healed or not. If I stopped taking my medicine and symptoms came, I needed His Word, His harness, fixed securely around me to help get me safely to the other side. I knew that if I had His Word to stand on, I could face anything that would come my way without wavering.

I don't know how long I prayed, but I suddenly knew I

had to read Greg Mohr's *Your Healing Door* book. I opened it right to a passage I had highlighted. It said:

> Every prayer of faith, every step of obedience, and every confession exalting the truth above the facts is another swing of the sword of the Spirit that will eventually cut you completely free from that sickness and disease. Your 'suddenly' will come.[2]

Father said, "Today is your suddenly." I sat on the floor in silence for a long time just staring down the hall before it started to sink into my brain that I had really received my healing. I had really just heard God say that to me. I was really healed from the top of my head to the tips of my toes. It was a deer-in-the-headlights moment, for sure. I was shocked that the reality of the revelation had happened right then, but I'd known for months that it was already done. I knew I was healed, but the reality of it coming to pass felt "all of a sudden." The Word had been healing my body as I had been renewing my mind, and now, it was finished.

When it had finally sunk in, the floodgates opened and I began to cry. I was overwhelmed. I securely fastened the harness of "Today is your suddenly" around me and stepped confidently out onto the tightrope. I got up off the floor and threw all of my medication in the trash.

Sickness and disease in my body was finished just as Jesus said it was over two thousand years ago.

Psalm 119:89 (NKJV)

"Forever, O Lord,
Your word is settled in heaven."

CHAPTER FIFTEEN

Now What?

S o what happens now? Too many times testimonies stop with the sharing of the victory and fail to include what happens after the healing comes. Many people think after they receive their healing, that's it; it's over and they never have to do battle again. They think it will be smooth sailing from there on out, so they let their guard down. It's finally time to relax, right?

I believe this is why so many lose round 2.

They defeated the enemy in round 1, and they feel invincible. Unfortunately, many times the same sickness and disease they defeated comes back with a vengeance and takes them out. The truth is the enemy can steal your healing if you don't remain vigilant. He will sneak back in on you when you least expect it, and this is frequently right after you win the battle.

The after-story of my healing—what's been going on since March 13, 2014—hasn't been all rainbows and butterfly kisses, but my victory over sickness and disease continues to this day. I have maintained my healing, and I want to equip you to do the same.

In the last chapter, I had just thrown all of my

medication in the trash. I sat back down on the floor and turned to chapter 11 of *Your Healing Door* and read again about dealing with counterattacks. A counterattack is simply an attack made by the enemy in response to some action or event. In this case, that event was receiving my healing. The war for my healing was won in that moment, but there was still an enemy out there that didn't want me to keep what I had received, and he certainly didn't want me sharing it with other people. I needed to be prepared for whatever he might throw at me. Matthew 12:43–45 (NKJV) describes why we need to prepare for a counterattack:

> When an unclean spirit goes out of a man, he goes through dry places, seeking rest, and finds none.
>
> Then he says, "I will return to my house from which I came." And when he comes, he finds it empty, swept, and put in order.
>
> Then he goes and takes with him seven other spirits more wicked than himself, and they enter and dwell there; and the last state of that man is worse than the first. So shall it also be with this wicked generation.

Those clean, empty spaces need to continuously be filled with the Word of God even more so after you're healed. Saturating your mind with His Word is vitally important so that if symptoms come back to deceive you into thinking you're not healed, they won't find any room to reside in your mind. They might find temporary residence in your body, but if your mind is full of the Word of God, it will recognize and evict the trespasser symptom quickly. Those symptoms won't be there long before they realize there's no room for them to stay and they are not welcome in your body any longer. Don't give the enemy an inch of wiggle room to come back. An inch can lead to unbelief, and unbelief leads to nothing but trouble.

Because I had read chapter 11 from *Your Healing Door*, I was mentally prepared for a counterattack from the enemy when I stopped taking my medication on March 13, 2014. I knew the symptoms that would typically come when I didn't take my pills every day, so I armed myself with Scriptures that dealt specifically with those issues.

For example, confusion was the first symptom that would hit, so I was ready with three specific verses which were kept on the tip of my tongue. Putting them on note cards and carrying them with me at all times was an important tool because the confusion would hit so quickly and powerfully, I wasn't sure if I would remember the verses if it came. Even if one of your symptoms isn't confusion, I still recommend using note cards. Sometimes in the heat of battle, in the throes of a fit of pain or distress, it may be hard to remember even the simplest of Scriptures.

These are the three verses:

1 Corinthians 2:16 (NKJV): "For 'who has known the mind of the Lord that he may instruct Him?' But we have the mind of Christ."

Proverbs 16:3 (NKJV): "Commit your works to the Lord, and your thoughts will be established."

Proverbs 10:7 (NKJV): "The memory of the righteous is blessed." In context, this Scripture isn't talking about the

remembering kind of memory. It's talking about the com-
memoration of someone who has passed. But it was within
the content of this verse that Father spoke to me, and it was
exactly what I needed at the time. I am righteous; therefore, my memory is blessed. Out of context? Yes. Does it
line up with the Word? Yes. Was it powerful ammunition I
could use against the Enemy? Absolutely.

Fatigue always followed at a close second on the list, so
Isaiah 40:29–31 (NKJV) was always in the forefront of my
mind.

> He gives power to the weak,
> And to those who have no might He increases
> strength.
> Even the youths shall faint and be weary,
> And the young men shall utterly fall,
> But those who wait on the Lord
> Shall renew their strength;
> They shall mount up with wings like eagles,
> They shall run and not be weary,
> They shall walk and not faint.

I wasn't expecting anything to happen, but I was certainly prepared if something did. A day went by without
taking the medication. Then two days. Then three days.
Then two weeks. Not a single symptom. I didn't tell anyone
during those first two weeks that I was healed, not even
my husband. I didn't want a single negative thought to be
placed in my head. I needed to stay saturated in His Word.
I told my husband that if I seemed quiet or reserved, it
was because Father and I were working on something, and

that everything was fine. My husband is a wonderful man of God, but out of his love for me he may have expressed concern at the sight of symptoms if he knew I was off my medication. He knew all too well how quickly and powerfully symptoms could come, so after two weeks of no medication and no symptoms, I was confident he would be convinced of my healing.

It was wonderful to share the victory with him. I waited another two weeks before I told my family and a few close friends. Word of my healing spread like wildfire and soon everyone and their brother knew.

It wasn't long before the first counterattack came, and it was in the form of an old enemy—fear. As more people found out about my healing, I had thoughts such as, What happens if my back goes out again? What happens if the confusion comes back again? What happens if people start to think I'm lying, and that I'm not really healed? What if . . . what if . . . what if?

The pressure to *stay* healed was weighing on me. I knew I had to nip those nagging thoughts in the bud from the beginning, because if I thought on them long enough it would be an open door for the devil to come in and steal what I had received.

I asked Father to show me how to deal with this attack. I very quickly recognized that all of those negative thoughts were no more than a challenge against what I knew was true, that I am healed.

So it all came down to this: Father said I'm healed and that's all that matters. I needed to do what I had done all through my healing journey. I needed to believe His voice above all others. When those thoughts would come, I countered them with what He told me. I spoke His promises out loud and rebuked the fear. His Word had become a sure foundation in me over several months, and I would not be moved from it by an attack of fear. It is a choice to counter those negative thoughts every/time they come. To this day I have to be vigilant in defending my position, and I am armed with an arsenal of God's Word to protect the territory I've claimed. Since my healing, the enemy has tried to break my front door down many times. I've sent him running every time, screaming like a little girl, by speaking the Word that is now a living part of me.

The second and third attacks came months later in the form of symptoms in my body. I believe the return of familiar symptoms is the enemy's number one strategy in counterattacks. If he can make you believe you didn't really receive your healing, he's won.

Familiar Symptoms #1 Attack strategy

I noticed I was feeling unusually fatigued and mentally sluggish, and I was also having some early morning joint pain and swelling again. I told Father, "I know this is not the disease coming back in my body, so show me what it is so I know how to stand against it."

The first time the symptoms came, He brought me to the story of Jonah. (I knew it was His answer to my question because I wouldn't ever think to look in Jonah!) In chapter 1, Jonah was running from the call of God on his life and had boarded a ship that would take him far away from Nineveh, which is where God told him to go. God had other plans, though, and sent a big storm to stop the ship. After a series of events, he was cast into the sea by the men of the ship (Noah's brilliant suggestion) and was promptly swallowed by a great fish God had waiting to save him.

Jonah 2 is the prayer he prayed from the belly of the fish. I want to point out verse 8:

> They that observe lying vanities forsake their
> own mercy. (KJV)

As is normal, I had no idea what that meant when I read it, so I did what I had developed a habit of doing. You guessed it, I applied the four principles that haven't failed me yet: remove distractions, ask for revelation, pray in the Spirit, and keep the Word always in the forefront of my mind.

A word study showed me that *observe* means "to give heed to,"[1] *lying* means "a falsehood or a lie,"[2] and *vanities* means "breath."[3] Based on those definitions, "observe lying vanities" could be translated as "give heed to falsehood of breath"; in other words, paying attention to someone who is lying through their teeth. Jonah knew the plans God had for him to witness to the people of Nineveh. That was his word from God that he chose to stand on in his desperate situation. I believe Jonah was saying his current circumstance of being in the belly of the fish was nothing more than a lie, and that if he believed that lie he would have been abandoning (forsaking) the special mercy and blessing God had given him to fulfill his purpose.

Likewise, I realized I had a word from God: that I am healed from the top of my head to the tips of my toes, and

Excellent

that I would walk in divine health. *Now* I had a word from Him that the symptoms in my body were just lies from the devil in a feeble attempt to convince me that I wasn't really healed.

Every symptom in my body was nothing more than a mirror image of what I had experienced during my sickness.

The enemy had no new tricks, and I was on to him. He couldn't bring me down with a spiritual attack of fear, so he tried to deceive me with a physical attack of lies in my body. Once I recognized what the symptoms really were, I certainly wasn't going to believe a lying vanity over the Word of my Lord and Savior. They had no choice but to go. I had prepared for this moment by filling my mind with Scriptures to defend against attacks, so now all I had to say is, "It is written," just as Jesus said.

No fight. No struggle. No battle. No fear.

In the beginning, it took a few days for the symptoms to go, but as time has gone on and the revelation that symptoms are just lies takes deeper root in my mind, the symptoms go much quicker.

The second attack presented a new challenge. The symptoms were the same as before, but when I tried the same tactic as the last time to counter them, the symptoms didn't go. Something was different. As in the first instance, I asked Father to show me what the symptoms were and how to stand against them. I was preparing for another spiritual battle.

What He said to me was not at all what I expected to hear.

He said, "You need to change what you're eating." Huh? Surely I hadn't heard Him correctly, so I continued to pray about it. Again, "You need to change what you're eating." That just couldn't be right, could it? I mean, I'm healed so I should be able to eat anything I want, right?

For two weeks I struggled with what I had heard Him tell me and continued eating as usual. All the while I was speaking against the lies in my body and wondering why they weren't fleeing this time. One Sunday night, symptoms still raging in my body, He said to me, "Fine. Since you're not going to listen, now I want you to do a twenty-one-day Daniel fast and I want you to start tomorrow." Dang. There was no denying this was a direct order, so I started the fast the next day as He had instructed.

Within three days, all of the symptoms in my body were gone.

Valuable Lesson

I learned a valuable lesson: Not all bad things that happen in my body come from the devil, and not every attack is spiritual. Sometimes it's just because I'm not taking care of myself by eating junk and not exercising. Maybe it's from lack of sleep or taking on too many responsibilities. Father was telling me that, just because I was healed, it doesn't mean I don't have to take care of my physical body.

Here's an example: I look at food and cigarettes in the same light these days. You can't smoke a lot and not run the risk of getting lung cancer. Likewise, you can't overeat and eat junk all the time and not run the risk of being obese, developing diabetes and suffering many other things that come from being overweight.

You must take responsibility for the care of your physical body and stop blaming everything on a spiritual attack. (Don't shoot the messenger!)

In 2016, I participated in a two-week mission trip to

Uganda and came back home with a terrible virus. I was completely exhausted and apparently had let my guard down. I was so sick that, when Patrick picked me up the day I got back, he took me straight to the emergency room. I must have looked like death warmed over for him to do that (I know I felt like it!). When the ER heard me say that I'd just gotten back from Africa and was running a fever (among other ailments), they went into lockdown. They put me in isolation and, in their exact words, said: "Just get comfortable and the guys in black SUVs will be here shortly." They were referring to the people from the Center for Disease Control. Patrick and I just looked at each other and laughed. I felt like I was in a movie!

After testing everything they could possibly test, the doctor came back with the lab results. He started reading through the list of results. "Sputum: normal. Chest x-ray: normal. Nasal swab: normal. White blood cell count: normal. Red blood cell count"—wait! Did he say my white blood cell count was normal? My white blood cell count hasn't been normal since 2001 when my thyroid quit. Ha! So this little trip to the ER only confirmed the fact that I am, indeed, healed.

#boom #itreallyisfinished
#satanisazerowiththerimknockedoff

What the enemy meant for harm, once again, Father had turned around for my good. The enemy's plan for that sickness was to instill fear in me so I wouldn't want to go overseas again, which I know is part of the call of God on my life. Instead of instilling fear, it made me more determined than ever to go. I did learn a lesson from that illness though. It's so simple, I really needed someone to help me misunderstand it. I can't run my body into the ground. It *I need to hear this* needs rest. Even if we're busy being about our Father's business, we still need rest. After a week of rest, I was back on my feet and running again, the virus never to return.

Rest, controlling your eating and making exercise a *WISDOM* priority are not only good for your body, but they are also effective way to exercise your spirit over your flesh. Believe me, your flesh isn't going to like it, but the rewards will be great.

Those were just a few of the counterattacks that have come after my healing, but the foundation of defending against them all is the same. No matter what comes against you after you've been healed, it all comes down to standing on His Word and standing on what you know. When a challenge presents itself—fear, lies, symptoms, or whatever it may be—I do the same things I did when I received my initial healing. I go back to His Word revealed to me. I stand on His promises. I believe His Word over lies. I don't waver in the face of the storm. I will not be moved.

> *I know who I am.*
> *I know what I have.*
> *And I know how I got it.*

My healing came by the power of His Word and His Word alone. Nothing will ever take that away from me. Receiving my healing was not magical. It was not super-spiritual. It is not unreachable. I simply did what Father instructed me to do and believed every word He said. I had faith that if He said it, it was a done deal.

You can have the same results I had, and I want to

encourage you to keep fighting. Keep standing. Keep seeking Father with all that is within you. The only way you can lose is if you quit. The battle has already been won for you, so why quit?

That's worth repeating: *The only way you can lose is if you quit.*

The path of your own healing journey is before you, and the map to your destination is contained in His Word. Follow it. I know the first leg of my healing journey is complete, but another has just begun: the journey to walking in divine health. Do I think it's possible to walk in divine health?

Absolutely.

You may be wondering how I can so confidently declare that one day I will walk in that level of health and how I know that is His desire for you as well. My answer is simple. These are the words from my Father:

"You are healed from the top of your head to the tip of your toes, and you will walk in divine health."

He said it. That settles it.

ENDNOTES

Chapter 1—When Darkness Rules

1. Kenneth E. Hagin, *Why Tongues* (Broken Arrow: Kenneth Hagin Ministries, Inc., 1975).
2. Andrew Wommack, *The New You & The Holy Spirit* (Colorado Springs: Andrew Wommack Ministries, Inc., 2008).

Chapter 7—Let's Do This

1. Michael Yaconelli, *Dangerous Wonder* (Colorado Springs: NavPress, 1998), 14.
2. Blueletterbible.org, s.v. "bear witness," "G4828-ymmartyreō," *Strong's Greek Lexicon (KJV)*, accessed April 17, 2020, https://www.blueletterbible.org//lang/lexicon/lexicon.cfm?Strongs=G4828&t=KJV.
3. Blueletterbible.org, s.v. "understanding," "G4907-synesis," *Strong's Greek Lexicon (NKJV)*, accessed April 8, 2020, https://www.blueletterbible.org//lang/lexicon/lexicon.cfm?Strongs=G4907&t=NKJV.

Chapter 8—Promises, Promises, Promises

1. *Merriam-Webster*, s.v. "mindset," https://www.merriam-webster.com/dictionary/mindset, accessed August 15, 2015.

Chapter 9—The Beginning of Faith

1. A. W. Tozer, *The Knowledge of the Holy* (San Francisco: HarperOne, 1978), 26.
2. F. F. Bosworth, *Christ the Healer* (Grand Rapids: Chosen, 2000), 111.
3. Blueletterbible.org, s.v. "fully," "G4135-plērophoreō," *Strong's Greek Lexicon (NKJV)*, accessed April 8, 2020, https://www.blueletterbible.org//lang/lexicon/lexicon.cfm?Strongs=G4135&t=NKJV.
4. Blueletterbible.org, https://www.blueletterbible.org.
5. Blueletterbible.org, s.v. "dwell," "G3611-oikeō," *Strong's Greek Lexicon (NKJV)*, accessed April 8, 2020, https://www.blueletterbible.org//lang/lexicon/lexicon.cfm?Strongs=G3611&t=NKJV.
6. *Merriam-Webster*, s.v. "fixed," https://www.merriam-webster.com/dictionary/fixed, accessed April 9, 2020.
7. *Merriam-Webster*, s.v. "operative," https://www.merriam-webster.com/dictionary/operative, accessed April 9, 2020.
8. Blueletterbible.org, s.v. "quicken," "G2227-zōopoieō," *Strong's Greek Lexicon (NKJV)*, accessed April 8, 2020, https://www.blueletterbible.org//lang/lexicon/lexicon.cfm?Strongs=G2227&t=NKJV.

Chapter 13—Friday Night Fights

1. Blueletterbible.org, s.v. "glory," "G1391-doxa," *Strong's Greek Lexicon (KJV),*" accessed April 9, 2020, https://www.blueletterbible.org//lang/lexicon/lexicon.cfm?Strongs=G1391&t=KJV.

Chapter 14—Suddenly

1. YouTube.com, https://www.youtube.com.
2. Greg Mohr, *Your Healing Door* (Woodland Park: Healing Door Ministries, 2008), 71.

Chapter 15—Now What?

1. Blueletterbible.org, s.v. "observe," "H8104-shamar," *Strong's Hebrew Lexicon (KJV)*, accessed April 9, 2020, https://www.blueletterbible.org//lang/lexicon/lexicon.cfm?Strongs=H8104&t=KJV.
2. Blueletterbible.org, s.v. "lying," "H7723-shav'," *Strong's Hebrew Lexicon (KJV)*, accessed April 9, 2020, https://www.blueletterbible.org//lang/lexicon/lexicon.cfm?Strongs=H7723&t=KJV.
3. Blueletterbible.org, s.v. "vanities," "H1892-hebel," *Strong's Hebrew Lexicon (KJV)*, accessed April 9, 2020, https://www.blueletterbible.org//lang/lexicon/lexicon.cfm?Strongs=H1892&t=KJV.

Order Information

Rom 8:11

Pg 123+24

2 Cor 5:16
John 3:3-8
Gal 4:6
1 John 4:17

Same spirit that raised Jesus from the dead dwells on you.
the spirit is the TRUE me

your body is your home - it is where the H. Spirit Resides
seeing things that are not as though they are - ?

4 Things

Remove Distractions
Ask for WISDOM + Revelation
PRAYING IN The Spirit
God's WORD IN The forefront of Your Mind

Spirit Soul + Body <u>pg 113</u> = Polly.

your body is your home. It is where the Holy Spirit Resides
the same Spirit that raised Jesus from the dead, dwells in you
— The Spirit is the TRUE ME

Oct 2013 - change ⎫ 6months
March 13, 2014 - healing ⎭

CPSIA information can be obtained
at www.ICGtesting.com
Printed in the USA
BVHW071357161120
593415BV00006B/541